Praise for Sally Cragin
The Astrologica

"I LOVE this book. The words slip off the page like silk. I was entertained and enlightened."

—Penny Thornton, internationally noted
astrologer and former personal astrologer
for Princess Diana

"Sally Cragin has a talent for incorporating the celestial and the mundane with humor and with equal insight into personalities as well as into the wanderings of the stars."

—Clif Garboden, former senior managing
editor of the *Boston Phoenix*

ASTROLOGY
on the CUSP

About the Author

Sally Cragin (Massachusetts) is an astrologer and author who has published articles on astrology in newspapers across the country. She has written the astrology column for the *Boston Phoenix* since 1998, and can be heard live Mondays on WCRN-AM in the Worcester/Boston area. She is also a theater and arts critic for the *Boston Globe*.

Visit Sally Cragin online at
http://theastrologicalelements.blogspot.com/.

ASTROLOGY
on the CUSP

Birthdays on the Edge of Two Signs

SALLY CRAGIN

Llewellyn Publications
Woodbury, Minnesota

FIRST EDITION
First Printing, 2012

Book design by Donna Burch
Cover art: Zodiac wheel © iStockphoto.com/Baris Simsek, Texture © PhotoDisc
Cover design by Ellen Lawson

Llewellyn Publications is a registered trademark of Llewellyn Worldwide Ltd.

Library of Congress Cataloging-in-Publication Data
Cragin, Sally, 1960–
  Astrology on the cusp : birthdays on the edge of two signs / Sally Cragin.—1st ed.
      p.   cm.
   ISBN 978-0-7387-3154-4
1. Birthdays—Miscellanea. 2. Astrology. I. Title.
   BF1729.B45C725 2012
   133.5'4—dc23
                                                                            2011036033

Llewellyn Worldwide Ltd. does not participate in, endorse, or have any authority or responsibility concerning private business transactions between our authors and the public.

  All mail addressed to the author is forwarded, but the publisher cannot, unless specifically instructed by the author, give out an address or phone number.

  Any Internet references contained in this work are current at publication time, but the publisher cannot guarantee that a specific location will continue to be maintained. Please refer to the publisher's website for links to authors' websites and other sources.

Llewellyn Publications
A Division of Llewellyn Worldwide Ltd.
2143 Wooddale Drive
Woodbury, MN 55125-2989
www.llewellyn.com

Printed in the United States of America

Other Books by this Author

The Astrological Elements

*This book is dedicated to everyone born on the cusp
and those who love them.*

Contents

Acknowledgments

This book emerged from a chapter that didn't make it into my first book, *The Astrological Elements*. Trust me, this was a good decision! As I was writing about people born on the cusp, I realized many clients, plus folks who came to reading, were eager to read a book just for them. No one I met felt they were "exactly" like their Sun sign, or the adjacent cusp. So thanks to everyone who asked me: "So when is *that book* coming out?!"

Here is *that book*. It has been a long time coming and many thanks to my family: my husband Chuck Warner, and our children Christopher "T" and Jet Beatrix. I am so grateful for your love and support. And a big thanks to my mom, Janet Cragin, who supported this project in so many ways, especially helping to provide a slice of time, space, and quiet for me to get on with it. My love and gratitude to you all. Thank you also to Pat and Dick Warner, Anne, Pat, Jillian and Amelia Costello, my Ingwersen family, and Hal, Lucie, Austin, Colin, and Benjamin Cragin. Special thanks to Gemini cousin Susan Cragin for her editing skills. Thanks also to my "mom writer" friends who helped provide enthusiasm and opportunities for writing: Gayane Seppelin, Laura Douglas, and Sarah Klapprodt.

Thanks to Susan Lozier, the director of Fitchburg's Maverick Street Preschool, where Jet is a pupil. I was fortunate to write part of this book upstairs in a nineteenth-century schoolhouse with happy children, including my own, playing and learning downstairs.

I am fortunate to live in Fitchburg, Massachusetts, among artists, writers, dancers, and actors. Huge thanks to my friend,

Mayor Lisa A. Wong. Her leadership and advocacy for the arts make our city a creative, vibrant, and eclectic place to live.

Thanks to the late Clif Garboden, my longtime editor at the Boston Phoenix and a dear friend who helped midwife my column, "Moon Signs," back in 1998. I am grateful to have been his student.

Finally, thanks to those of you who let me interview you for this book. Cusps rule!

INTRODUCTION

Some Observations about Cuspy Signs

Do you feel betwixt and between? Being born "on the cusp" is more common than you might think. More than 20 percent of all birthdays are cuspy birthdays. If you're within that population and interested in astrology, you have an exciting research project. You get to become an expert on not one, but *two* signs.

Daunting? Not really. The system of astrology provides ample literature and data on each of the twelve signs, and signs have similarities as well as differences. In my first book, *The Astrological Elements*, I divided the twelve signs into their constituent elements: fire, earth, air, and water, each of which has three signs. I wanted readers to learn about those four elements. That way, they could see that fire signs initiate, earth signs acquire, air signs communicate, and water signs might live through their senses in a way different from the other three.

So prepare to immerse yourself into a fascinating brew composed of combinations of fire, earth, air, and water! I have tried to be precise about identifying when a sign concludes, and the next sign begins, but you should know that the "ingress" (moment a planet enters the next sign, in this case the Sun) day changes from year to year. Depending on your year of birth, you could literally be one sign or another, depending on the year in which you were born. Some of the signs are highly variable as to boundaries, so "cuspy" can refer to someone on the *very* end of a sign (28 to 29 degrees), or *just* barely into the next sign (0, 1, or 2 degrees). I have had some interesting clients with a birthday at the very end of a sign. It's easy to conjecture that when they were in the womb, they were determined *not* to be the next sign. Or that their mom didn't want them to be the next sign and, therefore, went into labor at the first possible moment.

Now, I've also had clients who are at zero, one, two, or three degrees of a sign, and sometimes their gestation ran a little late. Clients born at the end of a sign sometimes have growing-up experiences that make them seem older than they are, too. I've also had clients born at the beginning of the sign who show precocity in unusual areas.

What about extreme prematurity? As the twentieth century wore on, it became more and more common for premature babies to survive at thirty weeks, twenty-five weeks, and even less than half of their expected gestation. Now, that's a huge gap between what sign you *thought* the universe wanted the child to be, and the sign that the universe thought the child *should* be. My niece is a Pisces, and she was born at twenty-two weeks. So despite having been expected in May she is an absolutely classic Pisces fish: sensitive, appreciative, and empathetic toward the downtrodden, prone to procrastination, but also capable of great sympathy. I can't imagine her as a Taurus!

So whether you're born on the cusp, or you love someone born on the cusp, I hope you'll find useful information here. And let me know what you think. I spoke to dozens of people during the two years of work on this book and was always struck by how insightful cuspy folks are about their so-called "divided self." My view: you get twice as much of the good stuff, and half as much of the difficult stuff. But that's up to you!

—Sally Cragin, May 2011

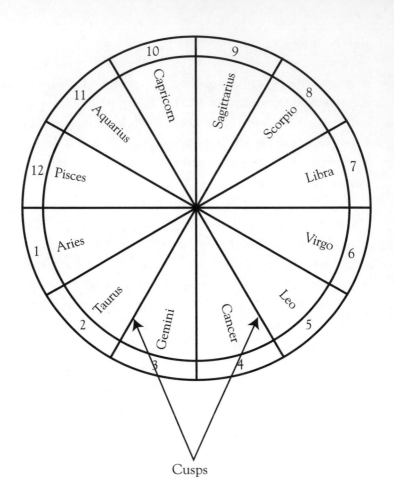

Cusps

chapter one

HOW TO USE THIS BOOK

Being born on the cusp can be perplexing, and can put you at risk of not thinking the astrological archetypes apply to you. For example, if you're born at the very end of Taurus, you might identify more with Gemini, especially if you can multitask (a Gemini quality) and also "take on more" (a Taurus trait). If you're born at the very start of Capricorn, you might have a Sagittarius sense of humor, interest in philosophy, or enthusiasm for biking, hiking, skiing, and horseback riding. If you're born at the end of Sagittarius, you might be more serious than your typical archer, who can be unruly and more easily vexed.

So which sign is the dominant one? I went through my ephemeris, which lists the angle of every planet for every day in the twentieth century, and confirmed that signs began or ended with a great range, depending on the year. Plus, the U. S. government altered the calendar during World War II so we had year-round Daylight Savings Time from 1942 to 1945. This presents further complications for those born during those years when trying to determine precise birth times.

Most newspaper daily horoscopes don't bother to give you the dates. Those that do might give the earliest possible date for the start, and the latest possible date as the ending. Yes, a bit confusing. The decision really is up to you.

To help clear this up, I've divided each cusp into three sections. For example, Aries-Taurus cusp is defined as:

- Aries, cusp of Taurus
- Aries-Taurus cusp
- Taurus, cusp of Aries

I've constructed twelve chapters that explore the twelve cusps in detail. You can read this book from front to back, but it can also be used as a reference tool.

Each cuspy section is divided into an overview of the signs:

- The Signs at a Glance
- Dates of Transition
- Details on the Cusp Aspects

After that, you'll find a section entitled "Lovers, Partners, Friends." Some people born between the signs get along superbly with people born on another cusp. Others gravitate toward those born in the middle of their sign. And a good rule of thumb for all is that the sign before or after yours is a good match.

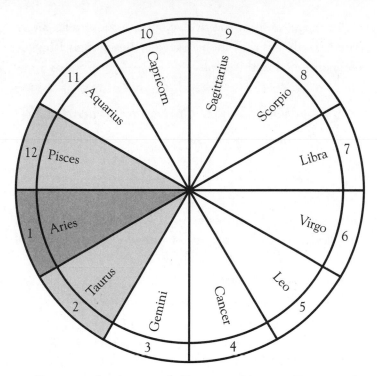

For example: Aries with Taurus and Pisces, Taurus with Aries and Gemini, Gemini with Taurus and Cancer, or Cancer with Gemini and Leo. You probably also get along with those who are *two* signs away. Aries with Aquarius and Gemini, Taurus with Pisces and Cancer, Gemini with Aries and Leo.

Each section also contains three lengthy discussions on each of the cusp zones. Because some of you are *definitely* at the end of a sign and some of you are *definitely* at the start of a sign and a bunch of you are "on the bubble" (e.g., on the cusp, could be one or the other), I include as much data and analysis as I can.

In the analysis of the twelve cusps, you'll find a directory of birthdays that includes celebrities along with people mentioned in this book.

A Few Words about "Careers and Vocations"

It is highly likely that in the course of your lifetime, you will change your job. Your interest in a particular field may shift, the economy may contract, or you may feel drawn to a path other than that for which you trained. All of us, regardless of birth date, or being born on the cusp between two signs, need to renew ourselves every seven years, and in variables of seven—so every 3.5 years, 21 months, 10½ months, and 3½ months!

Astrological clients have asked me time after time: What am I supposed to do? What should I do? To help you discover what may work for you, each chapter has a section on careers and vocations. I actually went through various directories of careers to get the specifics, and I surveyed my vast and interesting client base. You'll find specifics in the individual chapters, but I wanted to give you some "big picture" impressions as well.

I've found that certain Sun signs seem to dominate some occupations, and that certain Sun signs seem to occupy certain offices. In my experience, copy editors or proofreaders at newspapers or magazines tend to be earth signs, particularly Virgo (meticulous, painstaking). A social worker client noted that personnel in her office, which served families and children, were predominantly Sagittarians. I've known lots of Gemini writers, and many entrepreneurs born under Capricorn.

As I was writing this book, I met two Aquarius x-ray technicians (radiographers), both of whom were interested in changing careers. Teaching is a profession that has a variety of Sun signs but I've noticed that those who teach mathematics or the sciences—fields where there are correct answers and exactitude—tend to belong to the fixed signs (Taurus, Leo, Aquarius, and Scorpio). Those who teach language arts or history, or fields where there is narrative, interpretation, and analysis can be air signs (Gemini, Libra, Aquarius) or cardinal signs (Capricorn, Libra, Aries, and Cancer). I've noticed that those who rise to administrative positions can be earth signs (Taurus, Virgo, or Capricorn), because they follow the money; or Cancers, because they care about the group and keeping the group healthy.

The medical profession also has a wide range of temperaments and signs. Physicians who have had some time to select a specialty find it steadier going if they're an earth or water sign (Capricorn, Taurus, Virgo, Cancer, Scorpio, or Pisces). Therapists or those who specialize in disorders of mind or temperament can be in the Aquarius, Pisces, Gemini, Virgo, Libra realm. Now that's not to say that you won't be a good therapist with another birthday. But there is probably somewhere in your chart a planet or one of those signs at a significant angle.

The financial/banking field is rife with earth-sign folks, or those with heavy earth-sign influence. Those who deal with loans might have Scorpio in a prominent place. Real estate or mortgage specialists could have Capricorn, Virgo, or Taurus in a strong position.

Law enforcement, public safety, and the legal field are all over the map. Libra is the scales—often the scales of justice. I've known many folks in this realm of work who have Libra or Scorpio in a significant place. Cancer seems to be a sign for those who practice family law, whereas probate (other people's money) can be a Scorpio person's interest. Specialties in bonds or long-term portfolio investments could be Capricorn or Taurus.

Show business is another realm where every sign can thrive. In my work as a writer, I've had some excellent Virgo editors, and some fine water-sign editors (Cancer, Scorpio, and Pisces). In my work in television, I've met many fire- and air-sign people. TV and broadcasting media have very tight deadlines, requiring you think on your feet and learn on the job. Earth signs can do well here also, but they may have a longer learning curve, or be more comfortable in the editing or recording suite.

One huge advantage you folks born on the cusp have is that you understand the importance of having an open mind, being flexible, and being able to change gears.

Please note that in the next chapter, the birth dates for each sign indicate the *earliest* possible date and the *latest* possible date for each sign. For example, Aries can be born as early as March 20 in some years and as late as April 22 in other years, and Taurus can be born as early as April 21 or as late as May 23. There is no overlap of dates in the same year, but the dates when a sign begins or ends does vary from year to year.

chapter two

THE TWELVE SUN SIGNS

My editors thought it would be helpful to provide you with an overview of the twelve Sun signs as a starting point to this book. I write about the combinations in the chapters that follow, but here are some defining terms, along with my own observations.

- Cardinal means to initiate. Cardinal signs include Aries (marks start of spring), Cancer (marks start of summer), Libra (marks start of autumn), and Capricorn (marks start of winter). People born in cardinal signs are often excellent self-starters and can use their energy to start things moving.

- Fixed means constant and steady. Fixed signs are Taurus, Leo, Scorpio, and Aquarius, which represent months in the year when a season is in full swing—spring is in full bloom, or when the summer heat is steady, and so forth. People born in these signs are often hard working and determined; they can be resistant to change.

- Mutable means to adapt to change. Mutable signs are Gemini, Virgo, Sagittarius, and Pisces. The mutable signs represent the months when seasons change from spring to summer, or from fall to winter, for example. People born in these signs have the energy to transition from one state to another with more ease and adapt well to change, but they can also vacillate.

- A house is a designated area in the birth chart; there are twelve houses, and each house has a natural sign and ruler.

- Air signs are verbal. Communication and mental pursuits are their default modes.

- Earth signs are steady. Finding and using practical ways and taking on responsibility are their default modes.

- Fire signs are action-oriented. Adventuring out into the world and expressing optimism are their default modes.

- Water signs are sensitive. Attuning to emotions and perceiving the environment are their default modes.

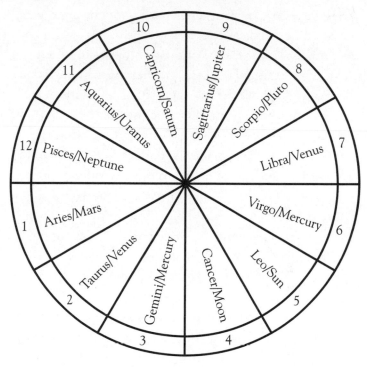

Aries
(March 20 to April 22)

The first sign of the zodiac—"the baby," as it were—is Aries. I've known many Aries who have that "baby face" look that can get them carded in a liquor store even in their forties! This cardinal fire sign is the first sign in the zodiac and is associated with the planet Mars. Aries' symbol is The Ram, and Aries folks can be "hard headed" at times.

Aries make excellent leaders, particularly if there's someone behind them with a dustpan and broom to finish and clean up what they have started. In my experience,

Aries are open to new experiences, excited by unexpected opportunities, and easily bored by routine. Aries can bowl over others with the force of their enthusiasm, which can add to their youthful quality. Yet, their bottom line is that they really do prefer the full approval of authorities.

Aries are known for their independent nature, and they don't always want to "clue" others in to what they're doing until they have made "it" perfect. Yet, they're often delighted to take part in an impromptu experience or project. Aries usually has a point of view about what you put before them; they can also blurt their opinion. They feel things immediately and are thus spared the fate of pointless brooding—a trait several of the signs indulge in.

As much as this sign likes a fresh start, folks born during this time can be quite canny at using experience or education from previous jobs to get to their next place in life. Aries is also curious (up to a point) about how everything works, so if you hire an Aries in your marketing department, don't be surprised if he or she ends up sniffing around in finance or Human Resources—just to see how things work. Pursuing adventure is always an interest, and since Aries is the ram that likes to climb mountains, people with this sign are natural climbers and want to see how far they can get.

In relationships, Aries can be highly loyal and somewhat volatile. They'll do well with a partner who will provide consistency and equal enthusiasm. From the summer of 1996 to midsummer of 1998, those born in Aries, no matter what age they were, experienced enormous growth and maturity. Yes, Aries can be "the baby" in their circle of family or friends, but there are times when they must climb more challenging mountains and that two-year period was one of them.

Taurus
(April 21 to May 23)

Taurus is the second sign in the zodiac. This fixed-earth sign is associated with the planet Venus. (Venus has a second home in Libra.) In Taurus, Venus brings our attention to personal security, banking, and valued possessions. Taurus folks like to say they're team players, and this is true, but only up to a point. There can come a time when they stop playing nice, and that happens when they feel others aren't playing fair or are being too bossy. Leadership and decision making are comfortable actions for people born in this sign, and they like to reserve the right to act like the boss when they feel they need to take that role. Represented by the bull, Taurus folks are slow to anger, but once riled they make formidable foes.

"Stubborn" is a word my Taurus clients often use when asked to describe how others view them. We have a good laugh, but Taurus is dead-serious about this particular character attribute. True to their fixed-sign nature, if they make plans, they like things to happen as planned. If they don't make plans—that's a deliberate choice. Taurus always gets tougher when they feel unreasonable pressure. If you ever need a support system to get through a difficult patch, Taurus will be there.

Possessiveness is another Taurus trait, but in my experience, their possessiveness is more about objects, advantages, or opportunities, and less about individuals. Taurus recognizes when others resist change. At their best, they appreciate this trait and honor it.

On the job, a Taurus is definitely the go-to person. Taurus folks will quickly rise to positions of responsibility in the workplace and *acquire* the accompanying tools, such as the security code and the full set of keys! Taurus likes to hear from others. They'll be sensitive to difficulties others have but not always willing to confront others. In relationships, Taurus folks are loyal and steadfast.

Gemini
(May 22 to June 22)

The third sign of the zodiac is Gemini. Represented by The Twins, Gemini has a dual nature (personality) that is typical of a mutable sign. Mutable Gemini folks adapt to change more readily than either cardinal- or fixed-sign people. Its element is air (like Libra and Aquarius), and it is in league with the planet Mercury. Like Virgo and Sagittarius, Gemini is a highly social sign.

When I meet Gemini folks in workshops, or at book readings, I usually ask them their thoughts on the "two-faced" part of Gemini. I question whether two personalities really covers the situation, and Geminis know what I mean. It's a sign that can go through moods at lightning speed. Geminis usually enjoy healthy self-esteem, a deep curiosity about human nature, and an ability to juggle projects like the comedy troupe the Flying Karamazov Brothers juggle objects.

Commitment can be a problem for them. They need freedom. Gemini can be wildly enthusiastic in an instant, and then change their minds and wonder why you can't keep up with them. I've seen a lot of Gemini people in relationships with partners who are much more stable, predictable, and conservative than themselves.

In their careers, Geminis enjoy opportunities to puzzle things out, to analyze, to work with changing groups of people, to be creative, to be free-form, and to be unpredictable. If you give them the instruction manual, they will do it their own way and never do it the same way twice.

Cancer
(June 22 to July 23)

Cancer is the fourth sign of the zodiac. This cardinal sign has the Moon as its ruling planet, and it is one of three water signs (Scorpio and Pisces are also water signs). Cancer is the natural tenant of the fourth house, which is associated with the home and family, feelings of personal security, or the need to be "well defended." Its symbol is The Crab. If you've ever watched a crab on the beach, you've noticed they can move sideways more easily than forward, and they avoid getting stepped on at all cost. Cancer folks I know will say they prefer to approach situations from the side rather than head-on and avoid confrontation whenever possible. When they feel threatened, like their symbol The Crab, they have no problem defending themselves. Cancer is associated with the stomach, and I've known many Cancers who have "stomach aches" when they're stressed, rushed, or feeling like others don't understand or respect them.

Cancers love their homes and are loyal, protective, and insightful. In their youth (which some Cancers extend deep into their lives), they love to travel and "try on" different personalities or "looks." I've met many Cancers who are naturally sympathetic—they are the first to say, "are you all right?" if you evince worry or concern. My Cancer clients are highly descriptive when it comes to defining and describing their emotions, which are deeply felt. Where Cancer gets into trouble is by making presumptions about others, and then being disappointed.

In a relationship, Cancer can be thoroughly committed very early. And if they get hurt, they get really hurt. Cancer people hold groups of friends together, and because they're a cardinal sign, they have true leadership potential. They can be social and solitary in equal measure, and they will usually describe themselves as more sensitive than you might think they are.

On the job, Cancers can be committed and passionate. They love work that requires intuition or curiosity about emotions and intellectual interests. They also love cooking (remember, the sign rules the stomach). They like to make their job their "home." In the workplace, Cancers can make it a habit to find out when others are having birthdays and plan the parties.

Leo
(July 23 to August 25)

Leo is the fifth sign of the zodiac and our second fixed sign (determined and persistent). This fire sign is prone to passionate outbursts and the occasional simmering sulk. Leo is ruled by the Sun, which makes it the "sign of kings." Ever notice how so many inaugurations and other ceremonies take place at or near noon? That's a holdover from ancient days, when early astrologers wanted to have the Sun, the most powerful planet, in its most powerful position, directly overhead.

Leo rules the fifth house, which is associated with children, public relations, parties, and romance. Its symbol is The Lion, and the part of the body Leo rules is the heart. Leos will often have thick, beautiful hair, and in my experience, Leos are frequently large-hearted and have a complicated relationship with their hair!

Leos are happy being the center of attention and don't feel fully alive without an admiring audience to applaud their activities. The ready smile (but not laugh) is theirs. Leos can sometimes be undone by hubris—by thinking that their private affairs are their own business. Some Leos can be very dignified in appearance and affect. Others can behave more like unruly kittens, made crazy by a dangling string.

On the job, Leos are sometimes uncomfortable if they feel they're too subordinate to others. I've known many Leos who rise to the top early in life. This can be a combination of natural ability, total dedication to the job, and an unwillingness to have others making decisions for them.

Others are often drawn to Leos—they're highly social. Leos likes to feel part of a "pride," and they also love to party. Leo friends will definitely be at the center of social situations, and they love the company. They're also fiercely loyal and encouraging friends.

Virgo
(August 24 to September 24)

Virgo is the sixth sign, and the second mutable sign. Virgos are adaptable, like the days during which summer transitions to fall. It's an earth sign (along with Taurus and Capricorn), and it is associated with the planet Mercury. Like Geminis, which are also associated with Mercury, Virgos are known for their curiosity and changeable temperament. Virgos are likely to have a perfectionist trait. Virgo corresponds with the sixth house, where astrologers look for information concerning health, work, and service. Its symbol is The Virgin, often shown as a beautiful female, surrounded by grain and other fruits of the harvest. Virgo oversees the lower intestine, and I've known many Virgos who carry "stress" in their lower intestine, so they have digestion issues.

Virgos can be smart and strategic, or completely undone by trifles. Because it's a sign that naturally "takes pains," it might take them longer than others to complete a task. Virgos don't want to be rushed, and they are excellent at analysis or finding a pattern of codes. They will not be happy if things are less than perfect. They can be generous to a fault, which emphasizes the "service" component of their traits and often includes needing folks or a cause to rescue. They can also understand underlying causes or conditions.

On the job, Virgos can quickly rise to positions of responsibility, once people see they're capable and willing to work hard. They like to work on their own, and they also like to feel they're helping others. They can figure out shortcuts, and they're wise about foreseeing pitfalls. Some find the process of working with deadlines exciting and necessary, while others like to work at their own pace.

Libra
(September 24 to October 24)

Libra is the seventh sign, opposite Aries (see figure on page 13). If Aries is about "I," Libra is about "we." A Libra is truly a partnership person. Libra is the third cardinal sign (after Aries and Cancer), and Libra folks often direct their initiating energy toward partnerships. Libra shares the planet Venus with Taurus. What they have in common with Taurus is a love of beauty, a taste for luxury, an appreciation of quirky friends, and a nose for investment.

Libra is represented by The Scales; it is the only sign in the zodiac that's represented by a "thing." All the other signs are represented by either a human or animal figure. The two kidneys and the ureters are the body parts that correspond with Libra. (One of the first things I say to female Libra clients is: Are you drinking enough cranberry juice?) The Scales also represent the scales of justice.

Libras are unpredictable. They reserve their right to change their mind, or change direction when they please, and others just have to adjust. Nevertheless, Libra folks make excellent friends and most of them are truly "partner people." They can adjust their own personalities to fit better with another—and they really don't mind. For a Libra, balance is their primary objective. They want everyone to get along, but they're also comfortable with some ambivalence, which is often their "default" setting. They will change subjects faster than Michael Jordan changed hands for a lay-up. Yet they love beautiful people, objects, and places, and will risk everything if sufficiently enraptured. It's just that they don't always know when they're enraptured.

Libras are versatile, which makes them great coworkers. However, they are in danger of being lead by whim, or by someone with a stronger personality.

Scorpio
(October 24 to November 23)

Scorpio is the eighth sign, opposite Taurus. Like Taurus, Leo, and Aquarius, Scorpio is a fixed sign (determined and persistent). All water signs are attuned to emotions, but Scorpio is the least overtly emotional of the three water signs (Cancer and Pisces are also water signs). Scorpio is associated with Pluto, and its symbol is The Scorpion. The parts of the body Scorpio oversees are the sex organs, or (if my mother is reading this) "organs of generation."

Charming but not overly sociable, Scorpios are charismatic, and occasionally devious with an ethical compass all their own. Scorpios are great gossipers, but they have to be in a mood to share since they really don't need an audience for most of their activities. Scorpio doesn't mind destroying and starting over—Pluto's influence of resurrection is part of their life plan. In my practice, I'm never surprised by Scorpio clients' long periods of inactivity, which are interrupted by some dramatic news casually shared: a divorce and a move; a complete change of career direction.

Scorpios can be blunt, and they appreciate bluntness in others, but they also reserve the right to be very sensitive. These heightened perceptual or sensitive abilities sometimes get them into trouble when they pair up with someone who is not as thoughtful or deliberate. At one of my library readings for *The Astrological Elements*, I asked people when their birthdays were. Wouldn't you know, the two Scorpios in the room—who did not know one another—had chosen seats on the aisle, in the back. This gave them a strategic advantage over the rest of people in the room. They could see everyone who had their hand up, and they could slip out when they needed to!

Sagittarius
(November 23 to December 22)

Sagittarius is the ninth sign of the zodiac, opposite Gemini. Like Gemini, Virgo, and Pisces, Sagittarius is mutable (adaptable, versatile). This mutable quality gives Sagittarians a certain flexibility and openness that most other signs don't have. Sagittarius is also a fire sign (energetic and optimistic), like Aries and Leo. Sagittarians can be risk-takers, and they have a great sense of humor, an attribute that is also attributed to Jupiter, Sagittarius's corresponding planet.

I always talk about the ninth house in connection with the tenth house (Capricorn's natural house). The ninth house is education; the tenth house is career. The ninth house is a journey; the tenth house is arrival. Sagittarius folks are more easy-going than Capricorns, but also more accident-prone. The part of the body ruled by Sagittarius is the hips and thighs. It is always entertaining to watch Sagittarians stride through life (with the occasional hurtle forward). Of course, sometimes they stumble, but they'll usually get up laughing. Most of my Sagittarius clients have bumps and bruises around their midsection from opening doors with their knees, or from awkward exits down stairs. Could this be because the symbol is The Centaur, half-man, half-beast? It's much harder to have six limbs to keep track of, not to mention a bow and arrow.

Sagittarians love a good joke, but their sense of justice is keen. They also tend to take people at face value, so they can sometimes be manipulated, or sold "a bill of goods." Sagittarius sometimes likes drama and conflict, and if they're "fighting" for a cause, or against a situation, they are feeling at their best. They usually have a lot of physical endurance and tend not to be brooders. Yes, they're emotional, but they can also move through their feelings quickly (which is a fire-sign trait).

I know many Sagittarius folks who pursue careers in the public safety arena. This sign definitely is happy in "rescue" mode. They may not need to heal others, but they like to help. They also will get indignant if you accuse them of too much ambition.

Capricorn
(December 22 to January 22)

Capricorn is the fourth, and last, cardinal sign, after Aries, Cancer, and Libra; and when Capricorn begins, winter is official. It's an earth sign, along with Taurus and Virgo; it is by far the most independent earth sign. Ruled by Saturn, long considered the heaviest and most potentially depressed planet, ancient astrologers always ascribed dread-filled auguries for poor old Capricorn, but in my practice, Capricorns can come out on top—as long as they keep their eyes on the prize.

The Goat is Capricorn's symbol—however, originally it was the "sea goat," or *Capricornus*. The parts of the body overseen by Capricorn are the knees, joints, and skin.

Capricorn is dogged, responsible, occasionally blunt, reliable, long-lived, prone to melancholy, and aware of being prone to gloom. They love to work on their own and are excellent entrepreneurs. Capricorns can self-protect by always vocalizing about how they expect the worst—that way, they avoid disappointment. Actually, I think Capricorn complains about the worst that can happen because they know how to fix things—if only they were left alone! They have one thing in common with Pisces: both are old when they're young, and if they're lucky, young when they're old.

Capricorns occasionally get themselves into odd love-muddles and sometimes need a lengthy period of healing and recuperation after a romance. But they can be thoroughly beguiled by their job or their hobbies, or may prefer the company of animals to that of people. If you're a

Capricorn, please give yourself huge leeway to be a perfectionist, a hermit, a zealot, or a couch potato. I've known dozens of Capricorns who are in leadership positions. You folks generally have no hesitation about being "in charge," and you're also willing to stay late and be the person who turns off the lights and shuts up the shop.

Aquarius
(January 20 to February 19)

Aquarius is the fourth fixed sign, and it shares characteristics with Leo, Taurus, and Scorpio; however, Aquarians are free-wheeling and fancy-free compared to the other three fixed signs. Aquarius is the third air sign, after Libra and Gemini. Whereas Libra and Gemini can be quite needy of partnerships—any partnerships—Aquarius folks are more independent and can go long stretches on their own. The planet that runs your life is the lovely, quirky Uranus. It's opposite the fifth house of children and parties. The symbol is the Water-carrier, but no, you are *not* a water sign! The part of the body it rules is the ankles.

If anyone tries to confine you—lord help them! Aquarius is the independent, maverick, visionary, don't-shut-me-in iconoclast, and we love you for it. Aquarius can be relentlessly non-materialistic, but still be quite sharp when it comes to money management. You love "what's next," and the language you use is the future tense. What's happening today isn't as interesting as what might happen next week. People who dwell in the past or that stew over resentments are interesting to you, but it's not the way *you* think.

Where others get into trouble with you is when they think you're more versatile than you are. You may resent others trying to change your mind, and possibly over-react. One part of being a fixed sign (and sharing a tem-perament with Scorpio, Taurus, and your opposite, Leo) is having settled ideas. Some Aquarians are good about mak-ing plans or setting a date for something to happen, but I've met plenty who prefer to "see what happens," or "not make a commitment." I have learned that some Aquarians want their invitation to an event that very day or hour!

You probably resist those in authority, and if you don't respect another person, it will be hard for you to stay at a job—you are the original "rolling stone." You also have enormous interest and sympathy for people who live with challenges. These can be injuries, disabilities, mental is-sues, or maturation problems. Aquarius is highly curious and likes to be surprised. You're usually really excellent at surprising the rest of us as well!

Pisces
(February 19 to March 21)

Pisces is the twelfth and last sign of the zodiac, the final mutable sign (after Gemini, Virgo, and Sagittarius), and the last water sign (after Cancer and Scorpio). It is sen-sitive and artistic, undisciplined, and old before its time. Neptune, god of the sea, is its ruling planet. It's easy to remember the themes that go with Neptune: denial, delu-sion, delight, deception. The twelfth house basically sums up aspects of all the themes in the previous eleven signs and adds a great big extra: secrets, past lives, and "what isn't seen." Pisces is associated with the feet.

When I do tarot card readings, using the zodiacal circle as the basis for the reading, I put out twelve cards in the place where the numbers on a clock would be. I always present the eleventh and twelfth cards—Aquarius and Pisces—together: hopes and wishes, fears and dreads. Pisces is a "heavy" sign, and the happiest Fishes I've met understand they are ruled by deep tidal pulls, and that they need emotional freedom and security before everything else. Sometimes that security includes solitude. Other times it includes playing Pink Floyd's *The Wall* over and over, or not making their bed because they can't wait to climb right back into it.

I've known many Pisces clients, friends, and some family members, and I can say there is absolutely no generalizing about this sign, the way I can say that Libra is always saying, "On the one hand ... On the other hand," or Leo fiddles with their hair, or Taurus is secretly proud of their stubbornness. There is one common marker: charming self-deprecation. Pisces has very complicated feelings and often takes the role of the person whom others confide in. Pisces folks are also easily persuadable, and sometimes they have a hard time saying no. In a work environment, Pisces will take on the tasks performed by others, and though they may grumble, they'll do a good job, even as they resent having to do it.

chapter three

ARIES‑TAURUS CUSP

The Signs at a Glance

Aries likes to start things and Taurus prefers to finish what has already been started. When you combine Aries excitability with Taurus steadiness, there can be a very strong will. These two signs together are very powerful. Think of a race car that has a variety of speeds, so you can go from a moderate pace to supersonic (depending on your motivation level). The two planets that combine here are Venus and Mars—a natural combination. Aries‑Taurus can be emotionally self-sufficient to a degree that may baffle more needy folks.

Dates of Transition

Aries ends on or near April 19. Taurus begins on or near April 20. This all depends on the year. If your birth date is April 19, you're definitely an Aries Ram. If it is April 21, you're definitely a Taurus Bull. The in between—cusp area—is that rocky terrain that both Rams and Bulls co-habit.

Details on the Cusp Aspects

Fire and earth are a powerful combination. Think of the combination as material (earth) plus a method of changing its form (fire), not unlike clay and a kiln, for example. You have definite leadership abilities and helpful attributes: tenacity, vision, and endurance. You also have more patience than most Aries. You can bide your time until it's time to act. Aries is about quick starts and initiation. Taurus is concerned with security, finance, and issues relating to "what you have" versus "what you are." Ask yourself: Am I stubborn? or do I have a stick-to-it attitude and confidence?

In my experience, people who have a blend of these signs thrive in the support of a group.

If you have a high threshold of pain, or the ability to be consistent in an exercise program, you're in tune with your planets, Mars and Venus. Impetuousness is also likely, although you will not be happy if others point this out. You like to think of yourself as decisive and directed. You don't enjoy or understand the dithering that makes air or water signs thrive. Your confidence might even bring a relish for conflict. Be mindful that you don't escalate a simple misunderstanding into a messy muddle of hurt feelings. Take the high road, when you can, and if others seek your advice (trust me, they will), the best counsel you can give is to let them discuss all points of view before weighing in with your summation.

If you're born at the end of Aries, you're probably able to make plans more effectively than those born earlier in Aries. You can see ahead to consequences, and you're more willing to wait for the support of coworkers or a counterpart before charging forward (people born earlier in April will presume they have support, but not necessarily check it!). I've told clients born at the end of Aries that they need to embrace their Aries energy, particularly if their due date was "supposed to be" in Taurus.

If you're born at the start of Taurus, you probably self-identify with Taurus traits—love of beauty, art, and music; stubbornness, resolve, and slowness to act. Aries gives you energy, drive, and the ability to do things differently than those born later in this sign. But you still like consistency.

Lovers, Partners, Friends

Aries-Taurus lovers don't necessarily have a "type," but they are prone to infatuation. The Aries impulse to "rush headlong" into an emotional relationship is muted by Taurus's more restrained nature. What I say to all my clients with birthdays in this area is that having a "dual" zodiacal influence means they can find happiness with a wide variety of people, but some will seem like a natural fit. For an Aries-Taurus, either Taurus-Gemini or Pisces-Aries can be a happy combination. You would share values, and in both situations, you would probably be the more consistent one.

Fire signs would add passion to your life in a way that could be quite dramatic. I've known calm Aries, Leos, and Sagittarius and choleric Aries, Leos, and Sagittarius. In my experience, you work very hard to keep emotions in check so you don't periodically explode emotionally. This is a spicy combination for you (particularly Leo). You could be kept on your toes—either dancing, or skipping as quickly as you can over the hot coals!

A relationship with a Taurus, Virgo, or Capricorn could also work out as long as one of you could recognize when-ever the relationship "got into a rut" (always a danger with earth signs). Solvency would probably come easily to both, but you could develop a taste for the "high life," that made for big bills.

Air signs—Gemini, Libra, or Aquarius—could be very exciting at first. They have so many ideas, and so many interests! However, one pitfall could be that you end up being irked or disturbed by their propensity for moving onto "the next thing." (This could be most maddening with Aquarius, which is at odds with your sign anyway.) As long as you're not perpetually on "cleanup duty" this could be a fun pairing.

Water signs—Cancer, Scorpio, or Pisces—might be highly satisfying and very stable in the long run. They'd bring a deeper understanding to the relationship; they'd explain and help you understand your own complexity. They'd be moody, yes, but that's when you could step in, and say, "Let's do this, and get out of the house." (Moody water signs are total homebodies, but they do appreciate when pried loose from the cave.) Scorpio would exert magnetism, but that's a sign that could be exactly opposite your Sun. You'd never fully know what was going on, and that could make for a feeling of being left out.

Aries-Taurus like consistency in a relationship. You want to know what your responsibilities are. Predictability is mostly a "plus" for them. However, some find that conflict is the most tempting battlefield, and failing to find passion in other arenas, they may look to a little jousting as the best way to fill in empty space. If you're drawn to people that you argue with, or who don't really seem to "see" you—you may need to rethink the parameters of the relationship. Because—let's be frank—you're a catch. And you've got a taste for success. You really do want to live the good life. So isn't that a treat for a partner also?

Careers and Vocations
Aries-Taurus

Accounting, airlines, antiques (dealing, restoration), apartment management, artist, auctions, automotive, banking, beadshop owner, beauty salon owner, cake decorating, golfing, candy and confection making, childcare (teaching, caretaking, tutoring), clothing/fashion industry, dentist or dental hygienist, floral designer, hairdresser, golfing, heating/furnace work, hotelier, hospitality, jeweler, interior designer, music teacher, optometrist, payroll, property management, plant shop owner.

April 15, 16, 17, 18
Aries, Cusp of Taurus

Childlike, but determined, these birth days make you a full-service Aries, with a touch of Taurus. For the most part, you like to start and finish projects. You can be stubborn, but you can multitask like a demon (unlike many Tauruses). You could be fascinated by sentimental relationships, and savor complicated personalities, or people who live on the edge. In general, the Taurus influence makes you want to feel "part of the herd." But the Aries side dominates, and you'll always step forward with ease and say, "Now, the way I see it ..."

April 17 folks include former USSR strongman Nikita Kruschev; writer, expatriate Isak Dinesen (who made Africa come alive for millions of readers); and rock promoter Don Kirshner (who had a brilliant idea, which was packaging the rock concerts happening at the Fillmore West into concert films, and later TV shows).

Having a good business-sense can be part of your story, but there's a notable exception: A&P heir Huntington Hartford. He was famous for putting his inheritance into a variety of "artsy" endeavors, including the amazing Huntington Museum and *Look* magazine. Hartford was excited by new ideas (very Aries) and he had great aesthetics (very Taurus). Yet, he couldn't quite put the pieces together to complete any worthy endeavors. The Taurus approach would be to endow the project, but in my opinion, Hartford was ruled by the impulsive Aries side. And, for most of his life, he had adequate means to make all kinds of dreams come true!

This birthday zone gives you more calculation than most Aries. You can see a few steps ahead, and probably have a sharp mind for thinking strategically. Clarence Darrow (April 18), the brilliant early twentieth-century lawyer, had this birthday. Darrow was a huge fan of the underdog, the long shot, and popular villains. (For example, he defended the murderous schoolboys Leopold and Loeb.) Giving people a second chance or the benefit of the doubt can be a strength to build on and sets you apart from other Aries.

Child star Hayley Mills also has an April 18 birthday. She's one of the few child stars who kept her equilibrium as she navigated adolescence and then continued with a performing career as an adult. Her most memorable film roles during her youth were girls with spunk and tenacity. You never saw her being shy or self-effacing.

I was fortunate enough to interview her in 2006, when she was appearing as the blind heroine Suzie in the thriller *Wait Until Dark* on Cape Cod. I was struck by the depth of her interest in the disabled. "I have enormous respect and admiration for people who brave the city and the traffic with a white stick—it's very courageous," she told me. Aside from the cultural assumption we Yanks have about the Brits and their "stiff upper lip," Mills' comments reminded me of how admiring of bravery Aries is, and how natural it is for the Ram to forge forward no matter what the consequences. And for Mills, it took a degree of courage to make films before, during, and *after* adolescence.

The path traveled by this Aries can be the rocky road of the mountain ram. One of your life conflicts is craving the (presumably safe) corral that encloses the (Taurus) bull. Meanwhile, as soon as you get some sense of the borders or boundaries imposed by others, your impulse is to do one of those mighty ram-like leaps and head up the mountainside that *no one* dares approach. Others may think you're more decided about a matter than, in fact, you are. You may need to learn caution and diplomacy so that you're not constantly saying, "That's not what I meant!"

You're playful and lively, constantly in search of "the new." You are also happy to bring your new find, trend, or experience to your circle of intimates. You're more adaptable than most Taurus-influenced people. You sometimes find your mission includes "making things simple" or "making things efficient." Taurus seldom stints on luxury, but you folks can definitely walk away from Taurus's need for "frills and furbelows." Your look can be sporty or minimal, and you don't mind changing your hair color and cut. You can take pleasure in small luxuries—especially if they're a tradition, like "girls' night out" or poker night. Your Aries maverick side won't feel completely fulfilled without a group of others to share your enjoyment. That's a really nice quality, and one your friends will appreciate.

April 19, 20
Aries-Taurus Cusp

What kind of beast are you? Depending on the year, you're a late Aries or early Taurus, and thus a true cusp baby. Your strengths are planning and building, and you probably have great taste (Paloma Picasso, April 19), rhythm (Lionel Hampton, April 20), and physical grace (Harold

Lloyd, April 20). Your drawbacks are willfulness and stubbornness, and you probably have an enormous capacity for enduring repetition or tedium.

Suzie Kowaleski is the animal control officer for the city of Fitchburg, Massachusetts, and she loves being an Aries (April 19). "I am very spontaneous," she says. "I don't need to plan things because I can just be 'go go go!'" However, there's a true Taurus flavor in her life because she is very consistent and responsible with the animals she rescues (and owns).

Some years ago, she joined Animal Care Education, an after-school program I developed with a friend, Dot Cassady. We bring information to kids about being a responsible pet owner. Suzie (with her dogs) has been a great educator. Her affectionate Venus-Taurus influence emerges with the kids and animals together. She says:

> When you're explaining something to a child, they have a spark in their eyes. They're really into what I'm saying and I love just watching their faces light up, especially when they are learning something good about being with the animals, like that it's okay to be nice to the animals, it's okay to be mushy. We open a window for them with that communication and how to treat them.

Sarah E. Collins is born just a day later (April 20), but she identifies profoundly with Taurus, despite having plenty of Aries influence. She's worked as a journalist and editor, and says her Taurus side includes liking "well-made, pretty clothes, especially vintage apparel, cooking, and consuming well-prepared food and wine." She dislikes change to her routine or sudden alterations, which make her uncomfortable with abrupt change, or the prospect of abrupt change. And, the classic Taurus obsession with abode passes her by:

> I'm less "house-proud" than some of my fellow Bulls. If I have disposable income, I tend to spend it on books, music, or clothes, not on slipcovers or curtains.

She's aware that Aries plays a role in her personality; however, she says:

> I have a short temper, I lack patience, and I can be quite verbally caustic and cutting (usually after the fact, not during the event/encounter that has left me feeling angry or impatient).

She's also aware that aspects of Aries are desirable: "I have a strong libido, and sometimes I wish I could be more 'Arien' about satisfying it." She explains:

> That is, I wish I could enjoy no-strings sex without feeling let down if I don't go on to develop a romantic attachment to my partner.

Others may have a difficult time understanding exactly what you're about—which makes for excellent protective covering when you decide *not* to put all your cards on the table. You really don't need the approval of others to move forward. Your charisma is blithe and deflecting—chances are, you're happy doing your own thing on your own terms and particularly on your own time line. You have tastes and inclinations deeper than many Aries, and versatility that most Taurus folks couldn't imagine. You also probably have a refined sense of humor with a taste for the absurd. Pratfalls don't do it for you, but subtle wordplay or Monty Python–style satire appeals to you. Your endurance is also awe-inspiring—others may describe you as "tough as nails," or "the Energizer bunny."

Of course, this cusp also brings an interesting (appalling?) array of villains: Lucrezia Borgia, the guileful poisoner of the Renaissance (April 19); Adolf Hitler; and Napoleon III (April 20).

As despicable as they are, we can learn from their example: rigidity leads to destructive action. To me, this crew suggests that a well-evolved Aries-Taurus person should continue to develop compassion and empathy, and not be lead by the nose by a self-created sense of dignity. Because you are ruled by impulsive fire and dogmatic earth, it may be tough for you to see subtle behavior tics others bring to relationships, projects, and interactions. A consoling mantra when things get out of hand could be this: "I don't have all the information right now."

I've found that Taurus's "conventional" side (that need for routine) is less developed with people with these birthdays. Aries' need to lead could be translated as "need to lead oneself." You're fortunate: you don't need followers to feel like you're leading. I've also seen people with one of these birthdays happily fly by the seat of their pants (not Taurus's favorite way to travel!). Taurus isn't really known for improvisation (regularity is so comforting), but you can perform under pressure. You also have that Taurus "protective" impulse.

April 21, 22, 23, 24
Taurus, Cusp of Aries

The bull is fully present here. But so is the ram, as a spectral presence. Are you a take-charge person? Can you figure out the quickest solution to a problem? Having executive abilities early on comes with this birthday zone. And there is no greater exemplar of the April 21 birthday than Great Britain's queen regnant, Elizabeth Alexandra Mary. When her reign exceeded the previous record-holder (Queen Victoria, another person on the cusp, born May 24), there was little surprise but much admiration. Despite the tendency of her offspring to "drop clangers," as the Brits say, with frequent disasters and missteps in their personal lives, Elizabeth II finds strength in consistency, joy in fulfilling obligation, and has achieved a personal style that's been mocked for decades. (Ironically, her principal dress designer Norman Parkinson, famous for all those colorful shapeless frocks, shares her birthday.) If you're born at this time, be aware of a natural impulse to set your jaw and purse your lips when someone else is "nattering on" about matters you think they know nothing about.

Patience is a huge strength for you. As a result, you really draw strength from friends or like-minded companions to be fully "at home." Your loyalty will always extend to the group. Delicacy of expression may not be your forte (unless you have Mercury in Gemini, say). For you, the idea of hiding or concealing feelings seems insincere and unfair. If this leads to conflict, you're well equipped to stand your ground, although you'll be highly resentful if another person uses "underhanded" motives or techniques. You'd be really irked if a partner was constantly summoning events from the past, or combining separate events into an occurrence so that nuance is lost. And despite real potential for patience, Aries can give you a devilish streak.

Years ago, I remember seeing Barbra Streisand on an awards show paying homage to Shirley MacLaine. I hadn't known they shared a birthday (April 24). In any event, Streisand was talking in a very interesting way about how they are both determined as Tauruses. I remember turning to my husband and saying, "Have they ever been in a movie together?" Neither of us could recall, and when I researched both of their careers, I was surprised to see that they'd never shared screen time. But then, when you think about the two of them, it makes sense.

Streisand's reputation as a perfectionist was handled maladroitly by the press during the 1970s and '80s, and MacLaine also had a reputation for having very strong opinions about her art. They both rose to fame from small on-stage roles: MacLaine replaced star Carol Haney in *The Pajama Game*, in the mid-1950s and caused a sensation. Streisand stole the show in a relatively small role in *I Can Get It for You Wholesale* in 1962. Various Internet sources claim the pair spent their birthdays together every year. So maybe that's exactly the right amount of togetherness to preserve a friendship between two determined Tauruses!

Here's another quality I've seen with people in this birthday neighborhood. Others may perceive you as a "scrapper," someone who can really defend a position, and be consistent about the reasons why you're doing this, and the necessity of doing it *your* way. You may end up protecting others quite often, or find that frailer, weaker sorts gravitate to you because of your strong will. Chances are, you'll be happy with a few "little buddies" around to give advice to or to provide some stability. For a truly happy life, here are some simple rules. "Keep it simple and get the whole story." You're still a Taurus, and something red, to you, is a flag to charge. However, red might just be a napkin fluttering to the ground.

If you can combine that Taurus consistency and love of beauty with Aries' charisma and energy, you'll be a force to be reckoned with. Make time for your aesthetic side—seeing a new movie, supporting a new team, or visiting a museum for a new exhibition will recharge your batteries. So will spending time with people with similar energy levels as your own.

You may be unlike many Tauruses, in that you don't have hoarding tendencies. Er, I mean collecting impulses. But you probably have pretty good taste and a taste for luxury items. Knock-offs—like perfumes that come with a label explaining "If you like Chanel No. 5, you'll love this!"—don't turn you on. And neither does extreme frugality. You probably won't have financial or spending problems if you have sufficient helpful aspects in your chart—more earth, a little air and fire, and not a lot of water. You like what you like, and you don't mind waiting for it.

You have a curiosity about trying new things. Whereas some Taurus folks are happy in the same hair or clothing style, you don't mind changing up your look, or occasion-ally wearing "sporty" clothes. You're not a dawdler and grow impatient waiting for others.

Final Thoughts

Aries-Taurus people can feel tension between being impul-sive and being passive. You may not want the responsibil-ity of leadership, but you need to be careful about criticiz-ing or commenting on the abilities of those who do choose that role. If you are the leader, you need to be very mindful of including others and letting them develop at their own pace. Aries can be inspirational to others, whereas the Taurus influence can be nurturing and gentle. You're pow-erful in your unique ways, due to that fire-earth influence, and others should not underestimate you.

Times of the year when you're "on fire" and should move all projects forward
February 15–23, April 17–24, June 19–25, August 21–27, December 18–26

Times of the year when you may feel compromised or that your judgment isn't as sound as you'd like
January 18–24, July 20–26, October 21–28

chapter four

TAURUS - GEMINI CUSP

The Signs at a Glance

Taurus is a team player, while Gemini is a utility infielder—able to play a variety of positions. Taurus consistency gets spiced up with Gemini's need to keep moving and keep things interesting for themselves. Taurus can bring a conservative influence, while Gemini is more freewheeling and willing to try something new. Here, friend-making Venus has a partner in curious Mercury. These signs together can make for a creative spark that others envy, along with the ability to follow through and get the job done.

Dates of Transition

Taurus continues through May 20 or 21 and Gemini starts around May 22, depending on the year. Therefore, those of you born on May 20 are Taurus, and those born May 21 or 22 could be either Gemini or Taurus, while those born on May 23 are definitely Gemini with Taurus influence. The Bull and The Twins evoke (in my mind) a "tag-team" of matadors taking on *el toro bravo* (the fierce bull). These folks have a personality that can provoke and be provoked in equal measure.

Details on the Cusp Aspects

Venus, which loves beauty and friendship, rules Taurus. Mercury, which is curious, changeable, and quick to communicate, rules Gemini. This combination of planets can provide fertile territory for an individual who's always passionate about communication and eager to analyze. Taurus's "Steady Eddie" proclivities get compromised, since Gemini concerns itself with "what if?" scenarios. The strengths of earth and air together are huge. You are a creative person; you can see a project through to completion. The "will o' the wisp" traits of Gemini can be diminished with Taurus in the mix.

Taurus's second house influence and Gemini's third house influence can be a boon for someone in customer service, or a job concerned with beauty or stability (galleries, banks, museums or theaters, credit unions) that needs a public face. Remember that Gemini wants to focus on messages—the more the better, and the more versatile, the "betterer"! Is that a word? It is for Geminis—adept mimics and wordsmiths. Your appetite for life includes huge tolerance for varied and unpredictable personalities. If there's any downside to this birthday zone, it's that your earthy practicality is weakened by airy effusiveness. Indecision and procrastination may result.

You love to be in charge, but you also need support from those around you. Taurus confers the aesthetic appreciation, while Gemini adds a radical risk-taking aspect. Do you multitask way more than a typical Taurus? Can you follow through more than the average Gemini? Are you stubborn and flexible, patient and spirited? Those are your paradoxical characteristics. Your biggest task in life will be to learn how to "lighten up" when others call you on inconsistencies.

If you're born at the end of Taurus, you'll like stability, but often get yourself involved with folks or situations that are inherently unstable. Your romantic impulses can sometimes make you gullible. You may be inclined to think others are more confident or capable than they are—just because *you* are. Gemini optimism and curiosity boosts your innate capability. I've seen a lot of imaginative and practical artists born on both ends of Gemini.

If you're born at the start of Gemini, you may be surprised at how comfortable you are with consistency, and "everything staying the same." You may not be able to see or feel that two-sided Gemini trait in yourself. Trust me, it's there! The wise person will make use of conflicting impulses. For example, if you feel like changing the look of a room, try pre-made slipcovers rather than having something sewn. This temporary solution can be a boon to those who need to mix up their environment.

Lovers, Partners, Friends

Loyalty and consistency count with you. Gemini can juggle, but your Taurus side definitely takes the upper hand. You're a romantic who's constantly surprised when others behave romantically. You're a skeptic after a romantic experience has gone awry—at least for a while. Your best partner is one who can counter your logical, analytical side with a tranquil "live and let live" philosophy. For you, lovers in the Virgo-Libra and Capricorn-Aquarius cusp may have some staying power. However, since you both have a measure of earth and air, you may be equally inconsistent. Other cusps could be Pisces-Aries or Cancer-Leo (these are long shots, but possible).

With your heavy Venus influence and Mercurial ambivalence, you might be fascinated by people who seem androgynous, or who haven't "decided" about their gender preference. Physical attraction is still paramount. I suspect your romantic journey will include plenty of "punched in the gut" moments from sudden crushes, and thrilling interludes where you lock eyes across a room with someone and find yourself babbling in mid-swoon.

Fire signs can be exciting but exhausting. Aries, Leo, and Sagittarius are fun, but do you have the energy to keep up? You know how much you hate that feeling of "losing control" if you're with someone who needs to dominate. (Leo would really clash with you). You'd counter their forcefulness with stubbornness and find yourself being in a position of "dousing the fire" periodically—for your own good and for theirs.

Another earth sign—Virgo or Capricorn—is a possibility, but unless they have a lot of energy, excitement, and curiosity, you might lose interest. These are signs that would be difficult for you to break up with. They'd make excellent business partners, however. And they'd also appreciate your opinion of them.

An air sign—Gemini, Libra, or Aquarius—would be quirky but interesting. You have a lot in common with Libra folks; however, air signs could be too flighty for your taste. You know what you like, and they often don't. Plus, air signs can cycle through a number of moods in an hour, and you'd be exhausted keeping up.

My experience suggests you'd be content with a water sign who can smooth over your rougher passages. I've seen your sign ally with Scorpio and Pisces. Cancer can also fit, but those born late in Cancer (closer to Leo) might be more enjoyable and less emotionally needy.

Chances are, you will end up being the "organizer" in your partnership. Taurus's influence makes you well suited to finding (or buying) a place where you and your partner can live. I've seen many instances of Taurus-Gemini cusp people who have their partners move in with them, rather than getting a new place together. But in the end, you need a partner who has patience when you need to double- or triple-check the locks; a partner who'll appreciate your ability to keep track of the bills and the books; a partner who will remember you put the laundry in, and even fold it for you.

Careers and Vocations
Taurus-Gemini

Accounting, advertising, small-animal care, antique store owner or employee, artist, auctions, banking, baseball batting-cage owner, beadshop owner, bowling, bookseller, bridal wear, cake decorating, childcare (teaching, caretaking, tutoring), clothing/fashion industry, costumer, dentist or dental hygienist, floral designer, golfing, hotelier, hospitality, jeweler, interior designer, music teacher, payroll, property management, sign maker, sound technician.

May 16, 17, 18, 19
Taurus, Cusp of Gemini

I can't figure out if you intentionally try to get the world to underestimate you, or it's just bred in the bone, but May 19 and 20 folks (still Taurus, but just barely) definitely have a "professional underachiever" veneer on a strong-willed persona. Sometimes you can convince others to believe this by creating an underdog persona that's actually a universal archetype. Think of Pete Townshend (May 19), who opined that his generation of teenagers hoped they'd die before they got old. Another musician who had a lot to say about his generation is Joey Ramone, the cheerful role model for self-identified pinheads everywhere. Spending time in "rock and roll high school" could be a pleasurable rite of passage.

If you're on this cusp, you could suffer from early-in-life self-esteem issues. Maturity is a great help for you—as it was for Taurus folks, who also have a Gemini skill with communication. Malcolm X (May 19) had a knack for incendiary language, and prolific French novelist Honoré de Balzac (May 20) was famous for exploring all classes of society. If your birthday is in this zone, you'll have a flair for language along with indisputable tenacity. Others may expect "brute force," but then they'll be disarmed when you charm them with specific language.

Loyalty is one of your traits. So is a taste for "treats," and for luxuries that may be the cause of occasional indebtedness. An appetite for "the deluxe version" could be a theme in your life, but you're no solitary miser and enjoy sharing pleasure with others. Having an audience is key, especially if they're radically different from you. Some Taurus-Gemini people are drawn to folks from a different (sometimes less advantaged) class than their own.

You are persuadable—unlike those born earlier in Taurus. In the early 1960s, Dame Margot Fonteyn (May 18) was considering retirement from the ballet when she was paired with a newly-defected dancer from the USSR: Rudolf Nureyev. They clicked on the dance floor, and his emotionality and stupendous physicality was a gorgeous match for her lithe and elegant form. She immediately understood that here was the partner of a lifetime, and the pair of them danced to world acclaim for many years afterward. Dance fans for a generation were grateful that Fonteyn succumbed to her Gemini curiosity about working with Nureyev, instead of doing the typical-Taurus thing. What's that? Doing what you planned to do in the first place!

Yes, you can be consistent, but you can also change gears and try something new. We don't think of adaptability as a hallmark of the bull, who prefers that red cape to any other color, but in your case, novelty can intrigue. You can be as focused as any Taurus in a field of study or passionate vocation. However, you're not usually subject to tunnel vision; interest in one topic doesn't preclude exploring another.

Chances are, your aesthetic sense is well developed. You probably like harmony in color and design. Perhaps this may translate to an interest in interior design. You can find yourself obsessed by getting precisely the right (size, color, and shape of) couch for a room. That leads to rethinking the entire space. In which case, you've suddenly realized you could be a decorator. Taurus cusp of Gemini often has discrimination. Can you browse a stack of wallpaper books, but unerringly choose the right color and tone for a particular room?

Interestingly, all of your "nesting" instincts don't necessarily require socializing to set off "that perfect room." Earth signs are highly self-sufficient and can attend their own emotions—perhaps because they have a different relationship to "stuff." For you, Gemini is an influence, but doesn't stir up as much of a need for change as it does for Taurus cusp of Gemini. If other signs (particularly those of the water and air elements) find your self-sufficiency strange, it's because they may not understand you need less social stimulation than others do.

You tend to think deeply, you enjoy slowly unfolding projects and relationships, and you especially appreciate proximity. If someone is close (geographically, or just in terms of consistency), that counts for you. Earthy loyalty makes you someone others trust. And at your best, you can appreciate the "high flyers" around you, especially if they're accomplishing feats of social, physical, or financial daring that you'd just as soon not try. But you do enjoy being an audience and your listening abilities are very good, unless you're personally emotionally invested. In which case, you may need to interrupt more than once!

May 20, 21
Taurus-Gemini Cusp

This birthday zone could find you with horns or with a counterpart Twin. You have vision, and you have drive. And you love beauty. And then sharing it with the world. Taurus is a musical sign, Gemini loves words. Consider Richard Wagner and Fats Waller (both May 21). Each has created an immediately recognizable soundscape. You can't hear the swooping strings of "Ride of the Valkyries" without feeling a degree of tension; ditto the merry stride piano casually playful tune of "Ain't Misbehavin'." Fats Waller was a big man with nimble fingers—his piano frills on his compositions were trend-setting and ground-breaking. Yet there was a solidity to his musical style that was uniquely his.

Hearing music that others can't (or won't) appreciate is a hallmark of this birthday. I'm fond of ethnomusicologist Frances T. Densmore (May 20). She recorded hours of Native American music on thousands of wax cylinders. You share a birth time with folks who are pretty tough customers when they need to be: Israeli prime minister/war hero

Moshe Dayan and philosopher John Stewart Mill (May 20).

May 21 folks have a remarkable ability add a modern flair to traditional forms. They are also hard workers. Take Andrei Sakharov, Russian physicist and dissident author imprisoned for sedition. What did he do in prison? He wrote more poetry! Another unlikely writing hero is Alexander Pope, a dwarf but also a genius man of letters during the neoclassical era in Great Britain. Both men had huge deficits to overcome, but nothing stopped them. And no one has written more successful pulp fiction novels than Harold Robbins.

I've known actor/director Christine Robert, of Lake Sherwood, California, for decades. She tells me I'm the only one who insists she's a Taurus, with a May 21 birthday (she's 28 degrees of Taurus by my reckoning). She's worked in literally all aspects of show business, from directing and cinematography, to editing and videography, to the financial/legal end (working with contracts, releases, and paperwork that's a necessary part of all artistic projects).

Most recently, she has returned to the stage and live performing. I think of her as having the best of both Taurus and Gemini traits, and asked her to comment. She told me:

> I feel like a Taurus in my fierce loyalty (when I commit to something or someone, I'm in till the bitter end) and my attachment to my (very often correct) opinions and positions. A little unyielding (at least in my own mind) especially at first, but I usually play nice in the end. I am truly a people-

person. But some of that could be the natural Gemini curiosity, too. I get along very well with Taureans. Though can't think of any female Taureans I know. All men. Maybe that's the difference.

My Gemini influence is starting lots of projects and not always finishing them, natural curiosity, floating high above everyone else, looking around, playful, having fun, not naturally being grounded and not wanting to be stuck in anything. I love to know a little bit about *everyone* at the party. I don't ever want to focus on one thing, I always love to do many different things and I try to do them well but if I'm not a master of something, I don't let it stop me from doing it anyway.

The strengths of both consist of (Taurus) undying loyalty, friendliness, and the confidence of knowing I'm right, and (Gemini) enjoying variety, getting the big picture on a situation, acquiring vast stores of superficial knowledge.

Weaknesses are (Taurus) not knowing when to back down from a position right away—sometimes I have to get my ego bruised before I'll concede a point, and (Gemini) being so spread out in terms of resources and having mastery of only a few things, beginning projects and not always finding out how it turns out because I don't always finish it, not being grounded sometimes feels very self-destructive, alienating, and lonely.

And I've finally discovered that success comes from picking one thing and sticking with it—like *forever*. But I'm forty-five and it took me that long to figure that out. Duh! I was always [thinking], *Oh well, I've done that for a year or two and I didn't really net what I thought it would, so I'll just move on to something else.* I think that was always the one reservation I had about having children. What happens when I'm over it? There had better be a backstop because when I'm done, I'm done. That's it!

Most recently, she's taken up the study of American Sign Language (very Gemini). I always look forward to hearing about what she's up to, because she has a unique blend of both signs.

May 22, 23, 24, 25
Gemini, Cusp of Taurus

Yes, you're a Gemini—a rare Twin who can be just as delightfully unstable as others of your group. Yet Taurus carries a big weight. I've met lots of folks with these birthdays who could have the word "Reliable" carved in deep letters on their headstones. Here, Gemini is basically operating in first gear, aiming for second (versus the fourth, fifth, and override gear that a Gemini with a later birthday enjoys!). You like having all the information. You also like to ask questions, but you're not always comfortable when others do the asking. Your learning style may be slow-and-steady, but once you understand something, you really understand it!

Geminis do like to multitask, and you might need to "pair" your activities and get two degrees at the same time, have two jobs, or work two different shifts. That Taurus influence could make others think you're less flexible than you are, so make sure you are clear about your ideas, perspective, or philosophy, because people *will* presume with this sign. Speaking more than one language or communicating in more than one way (musical, artistic) will make you happy.

Taurus's association with Venus gets you interested in beautiful things—words, objects, and individuals. Gemini's Mercury influence inspires you to ask questions, gather information, and weigh consequences. Firmness of character can be a sticking point with you, and you'll want loyal friends because you value quality, consistency, and reliability.

Yes, those born at this time have a sentimental streak. You could enjoy idealizing family life. Just consider painter Mary Cassatt (May 22), who never married, was highly opinionated, held her own in the salons of Paris, and made an interesting career out of stunning mother-and-child portraits. She took the design elements she liked from the Impressionist movement (Japanese tableau, intimate perspectives) and created a body of work that still makes people "oooh" and "aaah." Her portraits were highly realistic, yet loving.

Another interesting person with a May 22 birthday is Laurence Olivier. Multitalented (actor, director, producer), Olivier definitely exemplifies the Gemini influence. More than anyone of his generation, he was a veritable Michaelangelo when it came to the technique of his craft; for example, applying false noses and prostheses, gaits, accents, and hair styles to create characters. Yet he was always blithe when asked about his approach, saying it was all acting! (Acting with the right props is a Taurus trait.)

Those who have May 23 birthdays are also in the company of some rich, tough characters—people with long transformative careers—such as Rosemary Clooney and Joan Collins. Clooney's unique, husky voice (a Taurus gift) and distinctive phrasing (Gemini's gift) captured fans during the immediate postwar years and subsequent generations. She had a memorable syncopated style that felt "lived."

Other female singers of her era were noted for their bell-like clarion soprano voices, but Clooney had more in common with African American jazz singers who sing from the heart. As for Joan Collins—can you think of another sex-bomb ingenue who had her greatest fame and success in her forties? *Dynasty*-era Collins defined an era, and an entire nation watched this evening soap with great relish and anticipation—mostly to see what stylish bitchy comment Collins' character would utter next.

"Tough and graceful" or "articulate and determined" sums up those born on the Taurus-Gemini cusp.

Final Thoughts

You folks get the best of both worlds—consistency, dependability, adaptability, and imagination. Think of Gemini as literally blowing air into your earthbound proclivities. Yet, you'll also be less flighty than Geminis born deeper into the sign. You'll strike others as someone who is willing to take chances and is open for novel experiences, but you'll also bring a practical and considerate side to most of your dealings. In my experience, the universe puts you in situations where you have to understand the folks you're dealing with, *and then* you subtly change the dynamic so you're operating in a more stable environment.

Times of the year when you're "on fire" and should move all projects forward

January 18–25, March 18–24, May 17–24, July 20–27, September 20–27, November 19–26

Times of the year when you may feel compromised or that your judgment isn't as sound as you'd like

February 17–24, August 20–27, November 19–25

chapter five

GEMINI-CANCER CUSP

The Signs at a Glance

When adventurous Gemini and comfort-loving Cancer unite, the head and the heart must be equal partners. Gemini-Cancer individuals can be sensitive intellectuals, who can sum up their own or another's feelings in precise language. Gemini's spirit of "oh, what the heck!" definitely lightens up Cancer's intensity. This cusp combination can be impulsive and grounded in equal measure. The Moon's moodiness gets lightened up with Mercury's quirky and curious take on the world. And you may be the person among your circle of friends to remind others to keep an open mind.

Dates of Transition

Gemini continues until June 20 or 21, and Cancer begins on June 22 or 23. The crucial celestial event here is the Summer Solstice, along with midsummer harmony of light and dark. If you're born on June 20 you are definitely a Gemini, and if you're born on June 23 you're definitely a Cancer. Born between these dates, you're a crabby Twin, or a divided Crab, depending!

Details on the Cusp Aspects

Air and water together can be effervescent and fun, like champagne, or amusing and ephemeral, like bubbles. Just remember that children adore bubbles! I've encountered few folks with this birthday who aren't fully in touch with their childhood experiences. Yes, you may be more serious or intense than your typical Gemini, but you're also more light-hearted than the average Cancer.

The preoccupations of Cancer include the home and the father. The influence of Gemini makes The Twins good communicators, fluent at short messages, and capable of strong relationships with peers, including siblings. Gemini is impulsive, where Cancer is reactive. A superficial reading of Gemini folks suggests individuals that claim to tell everyone everything, but actually strike others as having hidden motives. Their similarities with Cancer are strong. Cancer folks want to conceal everything, yet they feel as though they're forthcoming and vulnerable. Mercury (Gemini) and the Moon (Cancer) interact in a dramatic way. You could be someone who is always the unpaid "therapist" in your circle of friends, or someone who is willing to point out when a friend has been "dissed." (This is not always advisable. Why borrow trouble?)

You may also have romantic ideas about "how the world should be," and can often be quite sharp about seeing solutions or workarounds for difficult decisions that need to be made. Cancer is self-protective, whereas Gemini is curious about others. Cancers absorb stress in their stomachs (I've known lots of Cancers who get stomach aches when they feel threatened), and Geminis communicate. So if this is your birthday, work on being clear about your wants, needs, fears, and hopes, because the advantage of clear communication will always trump your gut-level insecurity. And remember: gut-level insecurity is a warning that something is off. Learn to acknowledge this, take action, and move on.

If you're born at the end of Gemini, you'll have Cancer's sensitivity and awareness of others. You'll know it when you step on someone else's toes and your perceptiveness will make you a loyal friend. You'll need some heavy-duty maternal and paternal protectiveness. If your early childhood experiences don't include a lot of warmth and acceptance, later adolescent and adult experiences can find you trying to capture a feeling of security. You may be drawn to people who come from what you perceive as a "happy home."

If you're born at the start of Cancer, you'll be more easy-going and more adventurous than many Crabs. Cancer is a sign that can have a peripatetic youth before putting down deep roots. You'll be one of the rare Crabs who may be able to laugh at their self (a huge advantage for this group of people, who are sometimes over-the-top sensitive). You'll also be a Crab who can nurture others, without being so totally invested in the enterprise that you lose sight of your own needs.

Lovers, Partners, Friends

I'm always interested to see the person folks in your birthday area are attracted to. You probably want a partner who's independent, loyal, bright, and sensitive. You like consistency, and someone who's a little whimsical. Gemini-Cancer birthdays blend intellectual/analytical and emotional/intuitive strengths. A partner with attention to detail (and the ability to burn through trivialities) would be a help to you.

Air/water people, like those in your birthday neighborhood, plus Libra-Scorpio and Aquarius-Pisces could be a little too similar for much staying power. You can like them, but find it hard to go the distance. You see, that Cancer influence (whether you're a Gemini or not) can incline you towards self-indulgence. You need a buddy who won't blame you for those occasional bouts of self-indulgence and wallowing. Though you may want to claim the right of changing your mind, you will definitely appreciate steadiness and consistency from those who share your life.

For fun, try a fire sign—Aries, Leo, or Sagittarius. Just be warned: you may need to share the spotlight. And for my money, Gemini-Cancer people have an intense need for attention on their own terms, and then terrifically secretive urges as well. Aries would "get" you, Leo would find you fascinating. Sagittarius would be present, and then ... gone. That's the opposite sign to yours, by the way, and though opposites attract, they can also separate.

Earth signs—Capricorn, Taurus, and Virgo—may be appealing, but they may not be mysterious or interesting for long-term relationships, especially in your adolescence and early adulthood. However, those born at the end of Capricorn, Taurus, or Virgo could be attractive. But there's a risk: you may feel as though you've met up with a sibling, rather than a lover!

Air signs—Gemini, Libra, Aquarius—can make a good friend, but your Cancer side is crying out for consistency and kindness. Those air signs can be very kind and sympathetic but you can't always count on that response from them! Also, they process emotional experiences more quickly than you do. You'll be stewing with them over their agitated response over some misdeed long after they've moved on.

Water signs—Cancer, Scorpio, Pisces—would be temperamentally compatible, and you would love their depth and sensitivity. A Cancer partner would make for a solid and satisfying match. You'd understand one another, but you may make them crazy with your own inconsistencies and peccadilloes. Be very watchful about a partner's temper—you definitely can go off the rails, but someone too tightly wrapped might be simmering long after the heat was turned down on your argument.

Careers and Vocations
Gemini-Cancer

Advertising, antique store owner or employee, bartender, beekeeper, bookseller, candy and confection making, campground owner, counselor (seasonal), computer programming, career counseling, cook (particularly baking), dentist or dental hygiene, diver, environmental fields, film maker, hotelier, hospitality, plumbing, sign maker, museum curator (or development person), tavern keeper, teacher (especially the arts, music, poetry, drama, dance, painting, sculpture).

June 16, 17, 18, 19
Gemini, Cusp of Cancer

You're sensitive, and alert to others' moods. You've got Gemini's curiosity and tendency to analyze and a strong sense of humor along with fierce domestic urges. Gemini's "two personalities" are present in your character, but they're a hidden attribute. Others may be surprised to find you're a Gemini because you have deep domestic urges and Cancerian pride about your domestic or luxurious urges. Charm probably comes easily to you and you have a chameleonic ability to "gauge your audience." Since Gemini is ruled by Mercury, and Cancer by the Moon, you probably feel things before you think them, which can make you seem brooding or moody to others. But you're really a Gemini, and as such you're capable of quick changes of heart.

Partnerships that blur the boundaries between work and love can be an important part of your life story. Here are two artists who are partnership-driven. Paul McCartney and Isabella Rossellini share a June 18 birthday, and a proclivity to be at their best when working with another. We think of the McCartney-Lennon alliance as one of the biggest musical events of the twentieth century. (Lennon was a Libra who was also prone to romantic/professional partnership.) But McCartney wasn't just partnered with John Lennon—he also worked closely with producer George Martin on all the Beatles records. McCartney's orchestral interests were developed in the control room, describing to Martin the emotional mood he wanted, and then Martin suggesting instrumentation (the strings in "Eleanor Rigby," for example) to fit.

The public went on a "blame Yoko" tirade when the Beatles broke up, but the sad reality was that both John Lennon and Paul McCartney had spent their youth and adult years solely working with one another. It might be argued that Paul traded one Libra (John, October 9) with another (Linda, September 24), but it is the nature of air signs to change their minds, their direction, and their passions.

Isabella Rossellini's romantic interests were undoubtedly spurred by her parents, film star Ingrid Bergman and director Roberto Rossellini. Her relationship with director David Lynch brought her a quirky sort of stardom in *Blue Velvet*. She also was deeply involved with director Martin Scorsese. Rossellini's varied career (writer, model, spokeswoman, performer) is Gemini in nature, but the passion and emotional fluency she conveys is definitely Cancerian.

Two June 19 ladies are known for their partnerships. Film actor Gena Rowlands did her best work with psychodrama auteur John Cassavetes. Of course Wallis Simpson altered the course of the British monarchy when she partnered with the then-Prince of Wales, Edward.

Gemini is definitely the dominant flavor for June 19 birthday girl Kay Williams Graves. For many years she worked as a writer and researcher for a variety of publications including the *Soho News* and *Money* magazine. These skills stood her in good stead when she began the adoption process for her daughter. "We adopted her from China, back when nobody was doing that," she explains. "In 1994, there was no Internet, just the phone and the mail. The stack of papers we had was over a foot tall by the time we got her."

For Kay, marriage and motherhood brought out her Cancerian nurturing side. "I love to bake, I love to knit and crochet, and I love my pets and my garden, growing herbs and vegetables." Until she was in her late thirties, she "never lived in any city for more than five years." Now happily settled in Savannah, where she has begun a small business designing and crocheting dog coats (you can find her work on Etsy.com), she notes changeability as one hallmark of Gemini.

"My husband will say, 'Let's go to the movies tonight,' and I'll change my mind. I change my mind all the time. When I go to a restaurant I never get what's on the menu. I want what someone else gets." I suggest that the "homebody" influence is definitely a Cancer characteristic, and she says, "I'm such a homebody—I *love* to stay home. When I'm left alone in the house the whole world stretches out. I could be under house arrest and it wouldn't be a punishment." Kay looks at being a Gemini as a privilege and an advantage. "I think Geminis *are* superior. We're arty and creative and fun and not stuck in one rut all the time!"

I first knew rock-and-roll writer AJ Wachtel back in the punk rock era of Boston rock and roll—the early 1980s. We reconnected during my research for this book when I found out this enthusiastic connoisseur of the loud and proud is June 19 Gemini. "I've always appreciated being a Gemini," he told me. "I relate to the duality. There's the AJ Wachtel who goes out to club and does rock and roll and there's also the AJ Wachtel who stays home and is a dad." Unlike some folks, who grow up and put away so-called "childish things," AJ is still a dedicated scenester who's loyal to his mates onstage. That loyalty definitely speaks of a Cancerian influence, I suggest, and AJ tells me "I was always about friendship and family. I grew up the only Jewish kid in our Italian neighborhood. And I'm still in touch with half my kindergarten class!"

June 20, 21
Gemini-Cancer Cusp

You are attracted to intimate relationships but sometimes find it difficult to reconcile the ability to be a good partner with your need for solitude and self-reflection. Gemini's cheerfulness is muted by Cancer's enjoyment of "a good brood," and Gemini's versatility is underscored by Cancer's depth. You're drawn to both lightness and darkness, simplicity and complexity. And you could strike others as a cypher, unlike, say, Taurus (who lays their cards on the table) or Leo (who has a more obvious need to connect with others).

Gemini-Cancers in this zodiacal zone have a charisma that can bring out protective urges in others. Jean-Paul Sartre (June 21) was well cared for by Simone de Beauvoir. Prince William (also June 21) has a Cancer's self-protectiveness along with an ability to play many roles (athlete, college student, soldier).

But don't forget: Gemini is the master communicator of the zodiac. You folks will always get your message across— even if you have to make up your own style of speaking (Cyndi Lauper, June 20) to do it. You have tremendous emotional endurance, thanks to Cancer, and determination. We all know Gemini can vacillate, but the Cancer in your sign makes you want to go the distance. You love to bloom where you're planted, and if you're a "shrinking violet," it's not for long. If you're a wallflower, it's by choice.

You have the domestic urges of the Crab, but you also have a lightness and humor about it. Recently, I was reading about Nicole Kidman (June 20), and how happy she is living in Nashville with her husband, country singer Keith Urban. One of the hallmarks of this cusp is that you understand the importance of "home," and you are able to make a home wherever you're placed. Having a resting place, and an abode where you don't have to talk, communicate, Tweet, or blog is a necessary component to your well-being.

Be aware that this birthday can also come with a generous helping of grudge-holding. This isn't the most appealing personality trait, and learning to "live and let live" could be a lifelong pursuit. But you should know that some practitioners can turn resentful feelings into art. Consider authors Mary McCarthy and Francoise Sagan (June 21). Both were tremendously successful at creating entire worlds that contained thinking, feeling personalities. The psychological and emotional detail in their written work won generations of fans across the world. In another artistic vein, Rockwell Kent, whose career as a painter encompassed illustration as well as oils, was a questing soul who eventually spent time in Greenland, documenting the culture and the landscape.

However, you aren't always emotionally "cool." Gemini-Cancer is soulful and wants to be sincere. Artifice is not comforting, the way it can be for Libra or Leo. You'll wear your heart on a sleeve in a way that self-protecting Cancer folks (or earth signs) wouldn't dream of doing. To do otherwise would strike you as lacking in truthfulness.

Which brings us to another key characteristic: integrity. We hear this word a lot, but let's consider what it means. Integrity means you stick by convictions no matter what the consequences. Crabs are masters at retreating into their shell when threatened, but if you have strong feelings about a person, cause, project, or injustice, you will not rest until you have done what you can to right it. I'm thinking of Stephen Frears (June 20), the British filmmaker whose 1986 breakthrough film *My Beautiful Laundrette* chronicled the relationships and tensions between the white and Asian communities in Britain. It prompted fierce discussion on the editorial page as well as the arts sections as it explored Britain's economic policies, racism, and other hot-button topics.

Those of you with a June 20 or 21 birthday can have the best of both worlds. Gemini's flexibility and curiosity, and Cancer's emotional depth and responsiveness. Though you may have the Gemini impulse to walk away from projects before they're completed, have faith that Cancer's need to see things through will help provide motivation.

June 22, 23, 24
Cancer, Cusp of Gemini

You early Cancers have a sense of social responsibility and an instinctive appeal to others' protective instincts. You definitely understand the responsibilities of being in a partnership, and you don't mind altering some of your own personality to fit in with others. Since Gemini rules the lungs and Cancer the stomach, I was amused to see that seminal choreographer/director/stylist Bob Fosse was a Cancer (June 23). The costume he preferred for his dancers (exemplified by his muses, Gwen Verdon and Ann Reinking) was coal-black leotard, sheer black tights, and high heels. The signature move in all of his choreography was a hip thrust in one direction, and the rib cage jutted in another, and then a sly cock of the head from the dancer. Fosse loved his dancers to wear a hat, so they could peer out provocatively.

You see the theme—the slightly revealed, mostly concealed nature of Cancer emotions can provide a lot of romantic ups and downs. Most people won't see your vulnerability; they'll focus on your Gemini influence (verbal dexterity, relentless curiosity, quirky spirit). As a result, you may need to learn self-protection in some of your relationships. And though you may not come off as shy, Cancer's reserve and dignity will be a trait.

Meryl Streep (June 22) is an excellent example of a versatile Cancer cusp of Gemini person. Has any other performer been so lauded for her ability to completely inhabit disparate characters and portray nuance along with character traits? Streep's intense work ethic is successfully united with a sterling reputation among her peers and subordinates. She's a movie star with none of the entitlement issues. She's also that rare performer who can nurture other performers. She can play the tragedienne and the comic. Virtually no other performer has a lock on that range of emotional depth. Diane Keaton comes close, but never is subsumed into character the way that Streep is.

So what to take away from Meryl Streep's career? First —do your homework. People will always think you're pretty bright (Gemini's influence), and they'll also think you're a deep thinker. So you probably will be taken seriously in all your endeavors. However, be aware that Cancer is also a highly defensive sign. Brittleness is sometimes a byproduct—and whenever you start feeling that tension, you should ask yourself: Do I need to be alone right now? I have advised Cancer clients (ruled by the Moon, please remember) that periodically they need to "molt." That sometimes the world starts feeling too closed in—and that it's important to recognize when you've outgrown your "shell," whether it's a job, relationship, or project. This is why it's important to have friends you can trust, and who understand your vulnerabilities.

You'll notice the arts are well represented in this category—with plenty of innovators as well as those who find a signature style and develop it. I certainly see Gemini's greater-than-usual abilities to carry on a conversation, or to withstand controversy (Clarence Thomas, June 23) among people with birthdays on this cusp.

Someone like Anne Morrow Lindbergh, whose perennially top-selling memoir *A Gift From the Sea* (June 22) is clearly written by a Cancer in acceptance that nature and appreciation of nature will save the day, but shows ability to Gemini's strong communicative abilities and can sum up simple ideas with a degree of elegance. In the June 22 realm, a quixotic but awesomely competent and varied artist is Meryl Streep. No personality is beyond her. But Cancer wins out. You folks will have periods of "waxing and waning," and might need lengthy resting periods to recharge.

Final Thoughts

Air and water need a certain amount of space, but they also really need to connect with others. You're social and sensitive, insightful and large-hearted. When you're at your best, you can put everyone else at ease as well as bring out the best behavior in others. This birthday period includes the Summer Solstice, which many world cultures view as one of the significant turning points in the year. There will be times when you tune in to your "Gemini chatterbox" side, and periods when the silent and moody Cancer emotions take over. Learn to recognize this duality and embrace it—and keep your sense of humor at all costs!

Times of the year when you're "on fire" and should move all projects forward

February 17–24, April 18–24, June 19–25, August 21–27, October 21–27

Times of the year when you may feel compromised or that your judgment isn't as sound as you'd like

March 18–24, September 20–26, December 21–26

chapter six

CANCER-LEO CUSP

The Signs at a Glance

Cancer and Leo is, for this astrologer, one of the more interesting celestial collisions. The two largest entities in the solar system—Moon and Sun—meet for Cancer-Leo. Perceptiveness and decisiveness, empathy for the underdog and executive ability to get the job done may be the result. Often, there's a strong sense of humor—especially if there's an audience. Cancer-Leo definitely is sensitive enough to want to make sure the audience "gets" the job.

Dates of Transition

The Sun stays in Cancer through July 21 or 22. It moves into Leo on July 23 or sometimes on July 24. If you're born on July 21, you're a Cancer, and if you're born on July 24, you're a Leo, so those three days in between produce some interesting (and fierce) personalities. Imagine a Crab that attacks, or a Lion that's shy.

Details on the Cusp Aspects

This water/fire combination can produce hot water (or steam) a delicious stew, or in the most dire of circumstances, cancel out both elements. Imagine a flickering flame burning modestly that receives a bucketful of cold water. You need a decent amount of fire to counteract that bucketful of water.

If your birthday comes at this time, you have some powerful paradoxes to reconcile: Cancer's sensitivity coupled with Leo's confidence; or Leo's eagerness to jump into emergency situations, or taking a leadership position, combined with Cancer's ability to "read beneath the surface" when it comes to others' psychology. An absolutely textbook example of this combination of attributes can be seen in German actor Emil Jannings' most famous role: the Professor in Josef von Sternberg's *The Blue Angel*. Jannings (July 23) plays a strong-willed and prideful professor who falls hopelessly in love with a showgirl, "the blue angel," played by a very young and *zaftig* (plump) Marlene Dietrich. His obsession leads to his humiliation, but he is helpless to stop himself. His ability to show vulnerability and arrogance shows the extremes.

Okay, you want the bright side of this birthday? Efficiency and insight, bravery, impetuousness, and loyalty. And we need look no farther than Amelia Earhart, pioneering woman pilot (July 24) to see these character traits in action. Earhart's disregard for conventional gender roles in the 1930s made her a bright shining light for girls with a taste for adventure. Cancer-Leo people are also excellent at inspiring others to join their cause and provide needed assistance.

From my perspective, the astrological combination of Sun and Moon in one person is intoxicating and charismatic. You folks are sometimes perceived as men and women "of all seasons." You're sensitive and confident, personally insecure, yet also great nurturers. Overall, you "feel" your thoughts and "think" your feelings. I've also seen a taste for drama—small events can quickly spiral into "epic" sagas, told and retold with ever greater relish.

If you're born at the end of Cancer, you may feel like you have wallflower tendencies, but you really don't. Sometimes it's fun to play other roles, or to "act" the part of the shy guy or gal. You won't be as sensitive and easily bruised as the typical Cancer, but you also won't have their self-protective instincts. You may hurl yourselves full tilt into risky (or risque) relationships for the amusement factor.

If you're born at the start of Leo, your need for attention (and adoration) from others is tempered with a desire for a private life. Whereas Leo has a terrific roar, you'll be able to modulate yours, and can therefore take others into consideration. This is a great blessing, and will get you a reputation for being warm-hearted—which will be absolutely true!

Lovers, Partners, Friends

This water/fire cusp craves passion. Though you may have your own built-in resistance to committing, you could be driven totally bonkers by a partner who asks for the same patience. A partner who doesn't seem to be fully present could get under your pelt, and itch like crazy.

Don't fall for the "sad sack." This sign has such deep passions that you may mistake depression for a range of emotion. "If you cared as much as I did, you'd feel awful too" is a terrible premise for a relationship. And beware of the partner who swoops in wanting to "save" you. (That's your role! Just kidding…) You have a lot to offer your partner, and if you feel like you've "settled," trouble looms (that Leo pride will find an outlet no matter what!).

Signs that share your elemental combination, the water-plus-fire equation, like Pisces-Aries and Scorpio-Sagittarius cusp, seem like an odd fit for you (but this is just my observation). If you are able to find true love, you may have to overlook a partner who's not terribly thoughtful. Consider partnering with an earth sign: Taurus, Capricorn, Virgo. They'd share your taste for "the good life." They would also, in all likelihood, be happy with you as the "star." In my experience, clients with Leo placed prominently in the chart have a hard time finding people who can celebrate their good qualities. Sometimes they need to go through a period of spending time with people who aren't "overawed" by their star power. What happens? The person with Leo in their chart feels underappreciated and then resentful.

With security definitely one of your needs, an air-sign lover—Gemini, Libra, and Aquarius—could make you feel unstable. That's not a deal-breaker and you certainly can have a lovely relationship with an air-sign companion, but there would be a period of "growing pains" that could put you on edge. Once you get past that initial "will you still love me tomorrow?" refrain, a solid and rewarding relationship awaits.

Water-sign lovers would also keep you on your toes. A Cancer would be a natural fit, or a Pisces that had their personal act together (not overindulging in the usual vices!). Scorpio would be the toughest fit—you'd find them intense and Mercurial, and you may need to be "inoculated" against the sign. (Scorpios think of themselves as very simple, very solid citizens, but they're not always the clearest communicators, and your sign needs to know what's coming next.) In the end, the best match for you is someone who appreciates your sense of humor and dignity, and doesn't mind letting you have the spotlight for as long as you need it!

Careers and Vocations
Cancer-Leo

Animal care, amusement parks and party centers, bartender, beauty salon owner, beekeeper, candy and confection making, campground owner, counselor, childcare (teaching, caretaking, tutoring), clothing/fashion industry, clown (this is a profession!), environmental field, physical fitness trainer, hospitality, hotelier, interior designer, landscaper, plumber, tavern owner, veterinarian.

July 18, 19, 20, 21
Cancer, Cusp of Leo

The Moon's nurturing instincts are lessened by the Sun's childish influence. Imagine the scenario of mother and toddler in the grocery store. "Want that!" chirps a determined little voice. "No," says the mother, and thus ensues the tantrum a few exchanges later. If this is your birthday, you are a Cancer with an ability to move forward (rather than sideways), and your need for reassurance contrasts with your ability to provide nurturing to others.

This is a super birthday for those in positions of leadership—or who want to be. You have that sensitivity that picks up on others' vulnerabilities, but you're also tough enough to have a vision and to push forward as needed. And, you don't always have to be the star! Sir Edmund Hillary (July 20) is given credit for being the first person to climb to the top of Mt. Everest, but his partner in the adventure, Sherpa guide Tenzing Norgay, was right by his side. Hillary never directly claimed to be the first. When he talked about the ascent, he referred to it as a "team" effort. John Glenn (July 18) is another explorer, albeit of the heavens. His best-known quote, "We have an infinite amount to learn both from nature and from each other," definitely exemplifies his Cancer sensitivity. I can't imagine an earth sign, like Capricorn, having similar sentiments!

Hillary and Glenn are also excellent examples of bravery in the face of unknown outcomes—Hillary for tackling the world's largest mountain and Glenn for journeying onto the space shuttle when he was in his seventies. Having guts and just getting on with it is a Leo proclivity.

These birthdays are close enough to the Lion that if you're born at this time, you may be a risk taker. Of course, there are risks of various kinds.

In the 1970s, I knew plenty of students whose rallying cry came straight from Dr. Hunter S. Thompson (July 18), the Gonzo philosopher himself: "Reality is for people who can't handle drugs." There's a sly humor there, and when we look deeply, we find another really interesting Cancer cusp of Leo trait. Most famous for the drug-fueled odyssey *Fear and Loathing in Las Vegas*, Thompson is seldom given credit for years of careful political reportage, all spiced with his trademark sarcasm. In his prose, he was a madman, but I remember my dad telling me about meeting Thompson in the early 1970s and spending an afternoon in his company at the bar of Jack's, a legendary jazz bar in Cambridge, Massachusetts. Apparently, Thompson spent his afternoon quietly drinking beer, telling stories, but not being raucous and wild. "He was not like those books," my dad told me. "He was very subdued. I got the feeling he could turn on that side of his personality when he wanted to."

At its best, this birthday neighborhood brings leadership and generosity as well as an ability to share a spotlight. Two gorgeous actors, Diana Rigg and Natalie Wood, share a July 20 birthday. Natalie was a much-pushed child star, but Diana became a cult figure in her twenties, starring opposite Patrick Macnee in the British series *The Avengers*. The closer the birthday celebrants come to the Sun moving into Leo, the more frequently we find a chameleonic side. Leo is a natural-born performer, and Robin Williams and Jon Lovitz (both July 21) created original characters who are a little bit bossy and brassy. You don't have to enjoy being the center of attention if you have this birthday, but you should get used to it. The universe has a funny way of putting Leo front and center—and sometimes likes to coax The Crab from its hiding place as well!

Voice artist/actor Jeff Van Amburgh of Massachusetts is definitely a Cancer (July 20). But he acknowledges Leo influences in his performing careers. "I love a live audience," he says. "Performing in front of paying customers is such a thrill. Knowing that the people sitting in the seats have paid to be there definitely makes a difference in the electricity," he explains. "Just recording in a studio isn't the same. I like to have people in the room."

So if you're born at this time of year, enjoy having your birthday picnic outdoors—subscribe to a theater or performing group, and get comfortable speaking around others. And don't be afraid to be a brat now and then! Sometimes, that really pays off! For example, Ilie Nastase (July 19) was the #1 ranked tennis player in the world, and gave John McEnroe a run for his money as the crown prince of tantrums.

"If you have confidence, you have patience" is a perfect Cancer cusp of Leo cusp quote. Believing in yourself is step one, because everything that follows is really beyond your control. And though I've known Leos who are initially shy, the benefits of being a lion are an interesting and lovable personality (at your best!). Knowing yourself, your tastes, and your crotchets is one thing, but having confidence will definitely get you through the toughest times.

July 22, 23, 24
Cancer-Leo Cusp

Ah, betwixt and between. This is the true cusp of Leo and Cancer and if one of these dates is your birthday, you could be either sign. So how do you reconcile such disparate influences: Cancerian sympathy, perceptiveness, and vulnerability and Leo's confidence, bravado, and need for attention? Dignity comes with this birthday zone, as well as delight in breaking boundaries and expectations.

Some amazing twentieth-century women were born on July 24: Zelda Fitzgerald, Amelia Earhart, and TV's "Wonder Woman," Lynda Carter. Lynda Carter was the first buffed-up female star whose TV show debuted shortly after the passage of Title IX, which ensured equal opportunities for males and females in school sports. We owe her a debt of gratitude for standing up as the first muscle-bound pinup. In the case of Zelda, it is difficult to separate her manic mental illness from her stylishness as a personality. Her Jazz Age sparkle had a dark side, as we know from F. Scott Fitzgerald's *The Crack-Up* and her own semi-autobiographical novel *Save Me the Waltz*. Sensitive and extroverted, Zelda could be glib about her mental problems but also capture the heart with the depth of her anguish.

Here is one of my favorite quotes from her. If you share her birthday, consider having this embroidered on a pillow: "Nobody has ever measured, not even poets, how much the heart can hold." Now that's a thoroughly Cancerian idea—the proposition that emotion is quantifiable, and then the recognition that some concepts are beyond measurement.

Then again, Leo also roars in Zelda. Here she is on persuasion: "We grew up founding our dreams on the infinite promise of American advertising. I still believe that one can learn to play the piano by mail and that mud will give you a perfect complexion."

If Zelda exemplifies a verbal and dextrous interior life, complete with wit and style, sauciness and seriousness, Amelia Earhart is taken up by every generation as an avatar of female pluck and courage. Weren't you moved the first time you heard her tragic and heroic story? Artists as varied as Joni Mitchell, Kinky Friedman, and Ian Matthews have written songs about her legendary career. Cancer rules the home, but home was the last place Earhart wanted to be once she got a taste of the air.

Like any Leo, she embraced her growing fame, understanding it was the price she would pay for being able to do what she pleased. She also made frequent comments about the roles of women at her period in history which are still astute decades later: "Women must pay for everything. They do get more glory than men for comparable feats. But, they also get more notoriety when they crash."

JACK 93.1 Los Angeles writer and radio host Tami Heide (July 23) understands she can pick the best of both traits. "I totally have the Cancer homebody, domestic, cooking, gardening, decorating side," she says. Yet her professional broadcasting career has been decidedly Leo-like. "Maybe the fact that I do radio speaks to both sides of the cusp," she muses. "The shyer, protected side is Cancer. The outgoing, 'mouthy' part is the Leo. I've always said that radio is intimate without being intrusive. And it personifies traits of both Cancer and Leo. You can't see me, so it's hidden, which is the Cancer trait. And it's broadcast, which is the Leo trait."

Another Leo trait for everyone in the birthday zone is a focus on hair or coiffure. Early in her career, Tami worked at Newbury Comics, an independent record store in the Boston area. Her fellow clerk was then-unknown singer and songwriter Aimee Mann. "My hair was *really* short back then," says Tami. "Because we would get so bored in the store, I'd just say to her, 'Let's cut our hair!'"

I remember visiting Newbury Comics when both Heide and Mann worked there. I knew that Aimee Mann was in a band called The Young Snakes, but before I'd seen a picture of her, I assumed Tami Heide was Aimee, the burgeoning rock star, since Heide was far more outgoing in the store, joking with customers, while Aimee seemed more shy. Another Leo trait, for those keeping track!

July 25, 26, 27, 28
Leo, Cusp of Cancer

Yes, you are a Leo, lucky you! You can meow, purr, prowl, and hiss with the rest of the big cats. But sitting on your shoulder, concealed by your mane, is a very shy, water-loving critter called Cancer the Crab. And Cancer wants to make sure that you fe-e-e-el everything very deeply.

Is this a good thing? Absolutely. Leo is a powerful sign, the sign of kings, and it rules the heart. Having Cancer, which rules the Moon, as an additional influence is a powerful feature. Just think: the most important bodies in the solar system are reflected in your chart. The Moon and the

Sun take turns in the sky (and, of course, share it during eclipses). Doesn't that make you feel special?

I think that the Moon's influence on your Sun sign probably gives you a little extra "juice" as far as having an enhanced conscience and mindfulness that some other Leos aren't fortunate enough to receive. My experience with folks in this birthday zone is that your Cancer influence will probably be overshadowed by Leo's need to speak, to express, to protect, and to receive attention. You can be a great advocate for yourself, but you can also advocate for others. But there are times (see below), when your feelings of vulnerability could be profound and destablizing.

Sure, you can be shy and self-conscious. You'll definitely need to do the "Cancer sideways shuffle" into a dark corner when you've had enough of society. But you know what? You'll be able to pace yourself more than other Leos. "Running on fumes" won't be comfortable. You're someone who makes a home wherever you go. Sometimes "home" can be defined as intimate friendships (see previous section on "Lovers, Partners, Friends" for more information).

There are tremendously bright and inventive individuals born in this part of zodiac. C. G. Jung, the other patron saint of psychoanalysis (and an enduring influence on modern astrology), was born on July 26. So was visionary filmmaker Stanley Kubrick, who did as much to bring the artform of filmmaking forward as D. W. Griffith, and Aldous Huxley. And if you need a little glamor, Mick Jagger, elfin frontman for the Rolling Stones, blows out his candles at this time also.

So what do you do about your Cancer mood swings? Unless there's some other issue going on, your moods are probably not too long-lasting and you probably can get yourself out of a funk by having company or getting out in the world. You may feel sympathy for rather than have affinity with other Leos—your need for attention isn't as great as theirs, and you'll also have a strategic insight into others' weak spots. This is a great position for someone in sales who deals with high-end luxury purchases or objects that people think of as investments rather than quick purchases.

You can be the impresario rather than the star, or a supporting player who ends up in the spotlight by dint of good fortune. The folks that I've known who are born under a "lucky star" tend to be Leo more than any other sign. Perhaps because Leo more than any other sign knows how to have a good time and, more importantly, the importance of *having* a good time. The best way to get yourself back "on the beam" is getting out in the world. You need only so much seclusion to be healthy. Then, it's back to the dance floor for another set!

Final Thoughts

Sun and Moon combine in you. No other heavenly body looms as large as these two. Together, Cancer and Leo represent a unique range of motion, emotion, and action. The Sun encourages you to take action. The Moon urges you to reflect on your actions; consider consequences, and think about the people and circumstances in your past, particularly those who nurtured you. The Sun and Moon show optimism and guarded optimism, and reconciling these two planets requires courage and smarts.

Times of the year when you're "on fire" and should move all projects forward
March 18–24, May 19–25, July 19–24, September 21–27, November 19–26

Times of the year when you may feel compromised or that your judgment isn't as sound as you'd like
January 18–25, April 18–24, September 18–24

chapter seven

LEO-VIRGO CUSP

The Signs at a Glance

Youthful Leo meets workaholic Virgo, and astounds the world with their versatility and ability to suddenly step up to the plate, or into the director's chair. How can one see the big picture and all those tiny details at once? It's a gift for Leo-Virgo, but one that can make them thoroughly batty at times. Learning how to power down is a life lesson, as the Sun (which shines on everyone) and Mercury (which can make brilliant calculations) come together.

Dates of Transition

Leo ends on or around August 23, rarely August 24. Virgo begins on or around August 24. Those of you born August

22 are Lions, and those born August 25 are Virgins. Those born in the days between have wildness mingled with modesty, and a feral instinct that constantly needs attention. Civilizing a Leo-Virgo is not easy; it can take a lifetime.

Details on the Cusp Aspects

Like the Aries and Taurus cusp, Leo and Virgo mingle fire and earth, both powerful substances. The Lion meets The Virgin here. There's a gorgeous tarot card, "Strength," which sums up this image. Remember the story of Androcles pulling the thorn from the lion's paw and making a friend for life? You folks have that loyalty built in. You can also have a lot of charisma and a child-like charm that endures throughout your life. But you can be vulnerable to the opinions of others. With that Virgo influence, you are your own harshest critic, but lord help those who identify what you have already seen as weak spots (finishing something in a timely manner, not rushing on the most important part).

Leo is a natural leader, while Virgo can be a leader who makes everyone crazy with their changeability and preoccupation with trivia. The lessons you all get to learn are how to trust others to get a job done and how to be happy doing what you *can* do, not what you *should* do. Every Virgo I've ever met seems *just* like the description: critical, a perfectionist, and obsessed with detailed analysis. Leos, on the other hand are about the "big picture," not the brush strokes. Lions are deeply passionate and enthusiastic, vigorous cheerleaders of others' love affairs. Unlike many Leos, who are happiest in a pride, you Leo-Virgo folks have a distinct need for solitude and recharging. Sometimes you need to be the kitten who watches the other kittens play with the ball of string!

Watch the volume of your voice—I've known lots of Leo-Virgo people who have tremendous projection. This isn't always helpful if you are trying to impart confidential information. Watch your boredom level. Earth signs thrive on repetition and predictability, but your fiery influence will make you less steady and more easily distracted. Enjoy the skeptical side the universe gave you, but try not to let it make you jaded about the important stuff, like family and work you love. Leos are trusting. Virgos would like to be trusting, but they really only trusts themselves. Find the happy medium.

If you're born at the end of Leo, you'll be more thoughtful and inclined to think about *why* you're so opinionated. You won't get bogged down in as many details as your typical Virgo. The heart will rule over logic, but you may need more emotional reassurance than those with a later birthday.

If you're born at the start of Virgo, you'll be more effusive and generous than other Virgos. You'll also have a taste for drama, performance, and public activities. You'll be curious and probably an expert in persuasion—for causes or projects that improve people's lives, and health in particular.

Lovers, Partners, Friends

I can't tell you how many times a Leo-Virgo person has done the following in my life: alerted me that my shoes are untied, or that a piece of writing is due, or that I need to send my astrological calendar to so-and-so. Or that I really should send a story to a particular magazine, or that a certain store has the style of backpack that I like. In short, Leo-Virgo folks can be a repository of minutiae about folks they like. As for folks they love, Leo-Virgo is a very tough audience. I can think of two long-term couples who either share a Leo-Virgo birthday, or whose birthdays are within a day or so of one another.

Others perceive you as social, and Leo's influence can make you want to be part of a group. This can be your actual blood relations, or a random assortment of individuals (folks in your workplace, in a worship congregation, or in a hobby group). You want to create families where you go. So, even though one-on-one relationships are fulfilling, you also need to be with diverse groups. Virgo's influence makes you curious about others, particularly folks from other countries. In love, Leos definitely roar here. If you let the persnickety, finicky Virgo side dominate, you may find yourself more alone than you'd like.

Fire-sign partners (Aries, Leo, Sagittarius) are exciting and lovable for you. You'd understand their temperament, and you'd want to share their passions. You might have the occasional blow-up, but you'd both understand that sometimes "clearing the air" is preceded by explosions. A fire-sign person would help you loosen up, and not be so complicated (Virgo's influence).

Earth-sign partners for your sign (Capricorn, Taurus, Virgo) would be reliable and comfortable. But they might not have that dynamic spice you need. This is a partnership for a more mature period. If you've spent time with fickle folks, an earth-sign partner would bring a calming influence.

Air-sign partners (Libra, Aquarius, and Gemini) would definitely spark your interest. They'd have interesting places to explore and they'd love to have a partner. However, you might be put in the position of being "the parent," which means you'd be the responsible one.

Water signs (Cancer, Scorpio, Pisces) will always try to understand you, which is refreshing but could be aggravating. You're an action-oriented sign, so the brooding, contemplative types would be sweet for a while and then a wee bit of a pain. When you're all set to try something new, they've just reached their "comfort zone," so being on the same schedule could be difficult.

Careers and Vocations
Leo-Virgo

Accounting, animal care, alternative health care, amusement parks, adult care, beauty salon owner, bookkeeping, bridal shop owner, childcare (teaching, caretaking, tutoring), clothing/fashion industry, computers, physical fitness trainer, floral designer, hairdresser, health care industry, interior designer, librarian, payroll, plant shop owner or employee, veterinarian, wedding planner .

August 18, 19, 20, 21, 22
Leo, Cusp of Virgo

Stirring things up comes easy to Leos, who can barrel head-first into controversy and let others sort things out. You can have Virgo's organizational abilities (New York Giants' coach Bill Parcells, August 22) with Leo's courage. You may not be the easiest person to get along with, but when things are tough in the trenches, I'm sitting next to *you*! You're blessed with a degree of self-consciousness that is unlikely for Leos born earlier in the sign. You also are unlikely to put yourself on a pedestal.

Not all Leos are driven by fame, glory, and recognition. Here's an example. Years ago, I lived in Los Angeles, and happened to visit the China Club one night. This was a red-hot happening music scene, and that night Eddie Murphy, probably the most bankable movie star on the planet at the time, arrived. He was in a sleek black leather jacket, and was barely visible amongst what looked like linebackers wearing Italian suits. He caused quite a stir, as you can imagine. So the woman next to me and I stopped to watch this grand entrance. Then we resumed our conversation about early childhood education. At one point she stopped politely and asked my name. After I told her, she introduced herself. I'd been talking to Cindy Williams (August 22), erstwhile *Laverne and Shirley* star, who couldn't have been more down to earth.

Leo cusp of Virgo folks are more likely to ask questions than tell us what they think (Connie Chung, August 20). You can also have a reserve that Leos with earlier birthdays don't have. And you have an inimitable style that others may want to emulate. Coco Chanel (August 19) was transformative in the fashion world. Her work as a designer also helped change women's roles and how women were perceived. Her clothing was simple, stylish, and appropriate for both the work environment and socializing. And Coco's confidence, at least in public, was boundless. She is known to have said: "The most courageous act is still to think for yourself. Aloud."

You can find causes that change your life—and this can happen anytime. Sometimes fate intervenes, and the Leo cusp of Virgo person becomes the emblem or symbol of an event. Davy Crockett (August 17) wasn't the only frontiersman at the Alamo, but he's the one we remember. Robert Redford (August 18) liked to ski, and found that land was inexpensive in Utah. And the more time he spent there, the more he wanted to protect the region. A century from now, Redford will be remembered as an insightful and influential environmentalist who had a film career on the side.

Your strength is communication. Even if it takes you extra time, words, bits, or bytes! Your judgment will be treasured by others, so choose your words carefully. Sarcasm might be a temptation in youth—sometimes it's difficult to keep those Lion's claws sheathed! In maturity you will benefit from exhibiting "kingly" or "queenly" reserve. And a sense of humor is also a boon. Think of Ogden Nash (August 19), brilliant Canadian novelist Robertson Davies, and stand-up innovator Martin Mull (both August 18). Not for this birthday do we find the pratfalls. Instead, you should develop your deadpan verbal dexterity (that's

Virgo's Mercurial influence). You like words and how they fit together. A good conversationalist would interest you as a friend. So would someone who's innately curious about the world.

Probably the best-known Leo in this birthday zone is former President Bill Clinton (August 19). He, like Harry Truman, is the rare twentieth-century United States leader who came from truly humble origins. He made his way in the world by having smarts, ambition, and charisma. We've had many leaders who made a career in the military, and then made the transition to public service. But we've had only one president who was also a Rhodes scholar. Clinton's enjoyment of the public, genuine personal warmth, and tireless work ethic are Leo characteristics.

August 23, 24
Leo-Virgo Cusp

August 23 is the last date to be a Leo, and these folks can be unique geniuses. Or they can be artistic or cultural boundary crossers with pioneering impulses. My favorite drummer, Keith Moon of the Who, had this birthday. His shambolic and aggressive style was the perfect complement to band mates Pete Townshend and Roger Daltrey. Unfortunately, in his personal story, he was never able to access that Virgo precision. Stories about his narcotic and alcohol ingestion still set the mark for crazy rock star excess. Nearly a generation later, teen star River Phoenix, who shares that birthday, had his own odyssey of wretched excess.

But wait! Don't you want to access the precision that comes with Virgo's influence? You probably have an excellent eye for composition—"how things go together"—and you also have an artistic flair that's sophisticated, rather than simple. Endurance is one of your personal attributes. Some may call this stubbornness, but you're tough on the inside and outside. However, a sane and commendable example can be seen in genius dancer/choreographer/director Gene Kelly (August 23). I don't think this man gets enough credit for expanding on the dance tradition in this century. Built like an elegant wrestler, Gene Kelly was often airborne in his moves, suggesting the lion's pouncing ability. Yet if you were watching his feet, his precision and grace showed Virgo flair. He's an excellent model for anyone interested in the arts, sports, or public life.

Both he and Fred Astaire were genius dancers, but had radically different styles. Kelly was an athlete, and he was built like one. On the other hand, Astaire had the long legs and torso of a traditional dancer. Kelly brought a jazzy style to everything he did. In his career, I think that Virgo influence made him more curious about how things work, because he also became highly adept at camera work—the better to capture what he was doing.

So this is a wonderful cusp. You can access perfectionism, but if you're fortunate, you'll be spared the full-on Virgo need for control. Enjoy your Leonine bravery and joyousness, and take pride in the fact that no, you are definitely not an egomaniac!

One of my favorite writers in youth, Dorothy Parker, has an August 22 birthday. Parker was a groundbreaker in the world of newspaper writing back in the 1910s and '20s. She held her own with the heavy hitters at the Algonquin

Round Table, a group of writers and performers who gathered at the Manhattan restaurant for bibulous lunches and brilliant wordplay. She was the only woman who could consistently come up with toppers for punch lines, yet her personality was said to be shy and retiring, as she seldom spoke above a whisper. With Virgo as an influence, your wit has an edge, and a versatility.

You have an avid interest in different kinds of folks. But those who will always perplex you are the folks who seem to drift through life. Somewhere in your brain, there's a very high-function calculator that's always running, and the phrase "good enough" is enough to drive you bonkers. You want things to be as good as they can be—and if that means long hours, or taking over all aspects of a project, no problem.

However, Leo pride can get in your way. Consider the case of Shelley Long (August 23). She was the costar of a smoking-hot TV sitcom of the mid-1980s, *Cheers*. After several seasons, she decided the small screen was too small and that movies beckoned. She has had some excellent film roles, but her career didn't take off as she anticipated. My theory is that she is a genius at playing a comically OCD ingenue and the public decided that's how it liked her.

So, this birthday is that of the "fixer"—someone who can swoop in, determine what's gone wrong, and present a solution, workaround, or improvise a bandage! You are also versatile in your interests. In your professional life, choose a line of work that will let you grow, and move upward in the industry. You'll constantly be adding skills to your resume, because to let others do a less-than-perfect job is not comfortable for you. However, be conscious of how you speak to others. Watch your tone of voice, because some folks are going to focus on the "Leo" side of you. This means that something you say with confidence and certainty could be interpreted as you taking credit or looking for recognition. This may not be the case, but these are the circumstances where you'd be smart to pay attention to *how* you're saying something, not just *what* you're saying!

August 25, 26, 27
Virgo, Cusp of Leo

The turning point, the great divide—you Virgo cusp of Leo folks can cut to the choice, or present (and understand), numerous degrees of complexity. You're drawn toward patterns and human drama, and you can occasionally seem self-consciously emotional. There's a lot of versatility built into this birthday. Chances are, you have some mechanical aptitude as well as psychological insights. However, in my experience, you tend not to value or appreciate these talents as much as the rest of us do!

The zodiac can endow you with healthy self-esteem. But you may also present yourself in a mocking or self-deprecating manner. Why? Well, can you think of a better defense mechanism that can protect you from further scrutiny? If people aren't paying attention, you're free to do things the way that you want to do them. Others underestimate you at their peril because you folks usually come with a long memory. If you always cut your carrots on the bias, woe betide the helpful guest at your side who chops or dices for the salad. I've found folks in this realm (and in previous birthdays) are very averse to wearing bright colors (which is more of a Leo thing).

I think this is a difficult birthday to have because you can be torn between Leo's need for attention and Virgo's desire for precision. The attributes of Leo and Virgo are very far apart. If this book accomplishes anything, my hope is that those of you with these birthdays (and those who love you) will come to a better understanding of the complexities and challenges that come with a birthday that makes you want to chemically analyze the birthday cake even as you're singing "happy birthday" louder than anyone.

As August moves forward, those of you with birthdays on the 25th and later, definitely get tougher and tougher. You *are* a true Virgo but close enough to Leo to bask in reflected glamor and healthy self-esteem. Sean Connery has this birthday. So does Gene Simmons of Kiss and the first African American tennis champ, Althea Gibson.

There's an honesty to Virgo cusp of Leo. You probably have a, shall we say, less intense sense of personal vanity than Leo born earlier in the sign. Consider Sean Connery (August 25). He went bald early, but wore a toupee for many of those James Bond movies. By the 1970s, this down-to-earth Scotsman had had enough, and caused a stir by becoming the first sex symbol male movie star to go without his toupee in films. This, in my opinion, only added to his appeal, because of the honesty it shows.

If you have a birthday on August 26, 27, 28 and beyond, you might be called to be a benefactor. Helping others will be hugely rewarding. You're sharp when it comes to cause and effect, so you'll understand what a charity or nonprofit needs—you'll also see need where need may not be evident to others. The stellar example of this Virgo acuity is British social commentator Christopher Hitchens' archenemy: Mother Teresa (August 27). She, more than anyone, shows the power that a Virgo cusp of Leo person can do. As a young nun, she went to India, a country with an awe-inspiring amount of poverty. She looked for the lowest of the low (the untouchables), and decided that her mission was to help them. Her skill wasn't just that of a great healer; she was a brilliant administrator and promoter of the work she did. She was dedicated to making the world see the humanity of the population she served. No other missionary has even come close to having the global impact.

Yes, Mother Teresa is a tough act to follow, but take what you need from her story, which is the courage to speak up when there's unfairness and the dedication to communication that makes people notice.

Final Thoughts

You embody the Sun and Mercury. Openness and logic, overwhelming power, and changeability. This is a fun cusp, but it will pose challenges. Everything is "up front," with you as the Sun being the mightiest force in the solar system, and Mercury bringing intellectual sharpness. You have high standards for yourself, and approval of others is meaningful, but won't count for much unless you like what you're doing. You need more time and space to "do your own thing" than other Leos do. Make sure friends and family are close, and can help you be your best. You (along with Pisces) have an urge to "save" those who cannot be helped. Learn when to back away.

Times of the year when you're "on fire" and should move all projects forward
April 17–24, June 18–23, August 19–27, October 21–27, December 18–26

Times of the year when you may feel compromised or that your judgment isn't as sound as you'd like
June 19–25, September 20–26, December 21–26

chapter eight

VIRGO-LIBRA CUSP

The Signs at a Glance

Harmony can prevail when Virgo, the perfectionist, and laissez-faire Libra meet one another. But it's harmony that comes at a cost of indecisiveness at times. Mercury's curiosity meets indolent Venus (as it does for the Taurus-Gemini cusp), and sometimes it's a struggle to get off of that comfy couch and actually get on with a project! Just as with Taurus-Gemini, this cusp combination can process information quickly—usually before knowing what the actual feelings are about a situation.

Dates of Transition

Virgo finishes on or around September 23, and occasionally on the 24. Libra begins on or around September 24 or 25. Those born September 22 are definitely Virgos, with some Libra influence, and those born September 25 are Libras, with a Virgo twist.

Details on the Cusp Aspects

There's a lot of tension with the air and earth influences of Virgo and Libra folks. So much so that in your youth you can feel thoroughly divided. "Let's figure this out" is one favorite phrase, along with "Do we have to do it this way?" An essential instability and willingness to gamble comes with these birthdays. Your appetite for interesting people or possessions is similar to that of Taurus-Gemini. Virgo is acquisitive, but not to the extent of collector-maniac Taurus. I've known a lot of people with this birthday zone who are impeccably turned out and can put together an outfit without even trying. An instinct for harmony can be a benefit of this birthday zone.

Think of The Virgin holding up that set of scales and trying to keep them in balance. Practical and imaginative, driven and cooperative, this particular combination can make for a powerful personality and gobs and gobs of talent. These people may "feel" a particular Libra indecisiveness in themselves, but the earthy element of Virgo will propel them forward, regardless of self-doubt. Virgo can also add some "fine-tuning" impulses, so a really smart

Virgo-Libra person will ensure they always have friends around to bounce ideas off of. As for interests, I've known people who are business dynamos, or passionate about medicine (either research or practice). Others are artistic or in leadership positions in organizations or social groups.

Mercury makes you curious, and Venus can help you be a good friend or lover. Sensitivity about others' feelings is a strength. There can also be an "instant gratification" trait. Is it hard for you to wait to open your Christmas presents? Is your "trend sense" so sophisticated that the minute you close your copy of *Vogue*, you start fantasizing about this season's new silhouette? You might have a taste for symmetry and harmony, so the music of Bach or Mozart would appeal to you more than that of Stravinsky, or even Wagner.

If you're born at the end of Virgo, you'll be gentler, kinder, and more thoughtful than many Virgos who can be "all business" despite their enormous capacity for perceptiveness about others' motives. That Venus influence also makes you a good communicator with all—you can talk to people from all walks of life and also be a source of excellent advice.

If you're born at the beginning of Libra, you have turned the corner on the equinox and can settle down to work (and complete projects!) more than many Libras. You have a sense of judgment that is sharper than most Libras (except those with birthdays close to Scorpio). Mercury's influence on your Venus-ruled Sun makes you articulate, funny, and a good mimic.

Lovers, Partners, Friends

Graceful and thoughtful, curious and deliberative, the Virgo-Libra individual can be an excellent partner to all. You want to find common ground with everyone—no matter how much you may grumble. I've known people whose girlfriends and boyfriends range all over the map in terms of Sun sign. And in terms of a "type," you're flexible so you could be drawn to individuals who are more deliberate or decisive than you are.

You love to dress up to go out—looking your best gives you great pleasure, but you're open-minded enough not to require that your loved one exercise the same sartorial care. Partners who could mesh with you include Taurus-Libra, or Capricorn-Aquarius (I've actually seen more of the latter than the former). You have exquisite taste, so you would be attracted to the drop-dead gorgeous individuals. However, you have enough substance to give those who are "pretty on the inside" a chance.

Where you will need to be mindful in your relationships is keeping your own identity. The Libra influence gives you "the urge to merge," which doesn't just mean to make a partnership. For you, "merge" can mean taking on attributes, opinions, and interests of the loved one. The downside of open-mindedness is a porous personality. This can be a strength as you try new interests with a loved one. As long as you make sure your own personality, wants, desires, and proclivities get plenty of attention.

Fire signs (Aries, Leo, and Sagittarius) would be unpredictable and dynamic. Their tendency to "sweep you away" would be great fun at first. In terms of settling in for the long term, this element could strike you as unstable, particularly if you have financial challenges (highly unlikely). Aries is one of your opposite signs, and there could be a magnetic pull with The Ram.

Earth signs (Taurus, Virgo, Capricorn) would be stabilizing and fun. You'd share an appreciation for the finer things in life. And they would also bring out the practical Virgo side. You might find you're fussier around earth sign loved ones. However, you'd be financially solvent.

Air signs (Gemini, Libra, Aquarius) would bring out the Libra in you. You'll need to be careful with whom you choose because the tendencies of two air signs together is to say "whatever" a lot. This doesn't mean decisions happen very effectively. Just imagine taking a long trip together. Each of you is looking at the map, but can't decide the route. So you compromise and end up traveling hours out of your way for fear of offending. In this partnership, someone has to take the reins.

Water-sign partners (Cancer, Scorpio, Pisces) are loving and emotionally nourishing. They'd help settle you down when you get flustered, and they'd also remind you to take some time for yourself. Your domestic side would be well served in this partnership, and you'd be good for them. Their natural tendency to be moody or brood might be abrogated by your influence. Do opposites attract? Find out by making friends with a Pisces. Their free-form "let's see how I feel" approach to life could be a refreshing tonic, if you consider yourself "tightly wrapped."

Careers and Vocations
Virgo-Libra

Accounting, adult care, claims adjuster, health care industry, addiction counseling, alternative health care, apartment management, bead shop owner, beekeeper, bonds (bail and other bond services), bookkeeping, bridal wear or wedding planner, career or guidance counseling, computers, environmental fields, physical fitness trainer, floral designer, plant shop owner or employee, hotelier, hospitality, insurance agent or broker, jeweler, librarian, music teacher, payroll, property management, sign maker.

September 18, 19, 20, 21
Virgo, Cusp of Libra

Ah, equilibrium, where is thy sting! Libra is influencing you, so Virgo's tendency to analyze and dissect is definitely muted or diffused. You have a taste for precision and explanation but, if you're fortunate, you're more relaxed than Virgos born earlier in the sign. This can make you "results-driven" (not a bad thing to be). But you also don't mind the winding path en route to conclusion—or ending up at another destination altogether.

Now be warned: Virgos may regard you as more "flighty" than other Virgos. Your gift is flexibility, and the ability to say, "You know, I think I need to sit on that a little bit longer." So if decisiveness is difficult for you, make sure you have the time you need to do your work. You're a tolerant person, and you can be highly ambitious. But unlike other signs, you don't have to hit a bull's-eye every time.

Because you're a Virgo, "health, work, and service" are important categories for you. However, with Libra so close, you're more sociable and more understanding of the importance of being sociable than other Virgins. Even if you don't choose a medical profession to work in, Venus is close enough to your Sun that you'll nurture people in the workplace—particularly if they're on a deadline or need some help with a project.

You have a scientific turn of mind, but you also have imagination and flexibility that enables you to make leaps of insight. Other Virgos may see a situation as cut and dried, but you're more likely to see the shades of gray. Stephen King (September 21) is one Virgo cusp of Libra writer who is renowned for his productivity as well as "shades of gray." The career of this unique Maine writer has transcended the horror genre, and his dexterity with a variety of forms (novels, non-fiction, short stories, etc.), is a demonstration of Mercury's flexibility at its best. However, let's not forget the "cusp of Libra" part. Libra is so powerful a sign that it can have a dissolving effect wherever it's found. To this end, I'll suggest that the Libra influence on folks born at the end of Virgo is to give you a taste for harmony—no matter how unlikely or surprising.

This also means you'll be more of a "people person" than many Virgos. Cass Elliot (September 19) was widely acknowledged as the "heart" of 1960s pop group the Mamas and the Papas. Sophia Loren (September 20) looks like a queen but has described herself for decades as a down-to-earth wife and mother. In fact, while

I was researching this book, I had a difficult time finding egotistical or egocentric individuals born on this cusp. I think this is because having Mercury as an influence on your Sun sign, or prominent in your chart, makes you curious about others and willing to move on to the next thing. You'd probably be embarrassed by too much praise, and after you've heard one compliment, you've heard them all, so no need to keep going!

You like choices, as do all Libras (even if you pretend you don't). Mercury's influence can make you talkative, but Venus's influence can make you want to put a good face on what's being presented. You've got a really sharp mind for remembering trivia about others that you either find amusing or that you think might prove useful. Having "models" for behavior growing up is deeply meaningful to you. You enjoy trying on costumes, accents, and other traits to see what fits best. Others will find your comments insightful and discerning (even if you feel like you're dithering!).

September 22, 23
Virgo-Libra Cusp

These are the birthdays that put you in the crash zone of the wave, and people born at this time can sum up the impulses of the cultural influences and then turn out something that's brand-new *and* that has a wide, commercial appeal. This is no small thing. Being one step ahead (the way fire signs and Aquarians like to be) or blissfully wallowing in nostalgia (as the water signs, Taurus, and Capricorn enjoy) means you will hear things others can't.

There are some really wonderful musicians in this birthday neighborhood—artists celebrated for their integrity, authenticity, and grit. Joan Jett (September 22), the most successful member of the 1970s all-female glitter-rock band the Runaways, persevered with a musical career. She was on seemingly endless concert tours throughout the 1980s and '90s, and added to her fan base every time out. I speak as someone who saw some of her shows, which were brisk, no-nonsense, and completely captivating. Jett never exploited herself as an artist; she is a tough and accomplished role model for young women musicians worldwide. She may not be as rich or famous as Madonna, but she's a lot easier to like, and her image is gloriously consistent.

Some fabulous band leaders are associated with the September 23 birthday. These include John Coltrane, Ray Charles, and Bruce Springsteen. As "harmony" is a Libra concept and "intricacy" is a Virgo theme, you can see the similarities. Coltrane had awesome breath control as a saxophonist, and a mesmerizing talent for adjusting time-signatures. By taking standards and contorting the melody lines, he innovated a new sound and style. His sax playing was a natural outgrowth of bebop and free jazz, which was ahead of the curve.

Ray Charles is another innovator with awesome chops and self-discipline. He took influences from across the Western musical spectrum, from jazz to blues, to show tunes to folk tunes, and imbued all of his work with vitality. He was also one of the earliest African American artists to cross the color barrier before the Civil Rights movement. Bruce Springsteen is perhaps the last rock band leader whose ensemble includes a horn section (a staple for bands of earlier eras). Remember when *Time* magazine anointed Bruce Springsteen the "king of rock and roll"? That's because he'd brought the basics back to rock music at the height of arena rock. Springsteen's later work has been cited by both political parties for its focus on social justice, but the man himself thinks of what he does in simple, even primal terms.

When I was researching his career, I found a quote from an issue of *Doubletake Magazine*, in an interview Springsteen did with Will Percy, the nephew of writer Walker Percy, around 1995.

Springsteen defined the act of putting on a concert as presenting a gallery of portraits and ideas so that his audience can ask themselves the questions the artist is presenting. His desire is that the fans have "fundamental moral questions about the way we live and the way we behave toward one another—and then move those questions from the aesthetic into the practical, into some sort of action, whether it's action in the community, or action in the way you treat your wife, or your kid, or speak to the guy who works with you."

Okay, so you may not be a musician, composer, artist, or player, but consider this: the folks mentioned above all have enormous consistency and broad popular appeal. If you're born around this time, you have the potential to connect with an audience that many other signs don't, won't, or can't have. One question you may ask yourself over and over is: How real is this? How genuine? Phoniness is anathema, and you'll raise others' consciousness by how you handle individuals and situations.

Yes, this could be a huge responsibility. But you're well-equipped. Wanting to interact with others is a Libra prerogative; wanting to educate others is Virgo. Those of you in this birthday neighborhood probably have a responsibility—some self-imposed—and a compulsion to improve society. You have an important role to play in the world. So you may *not* want to take on this responsibility. However, I, for one, will be very curious to see what your passions are. The human desire to socialize could (with Virgo so close) always be transmuted into a work project or a project designed to "change the world."

At your best, you'll have the charisma that comes with curiosity, and the flexibility to speak to anyone. There's a chameleonic trait that's very subtle. Some folks never quite discover it, but if you're fortunate, you'll regularly put yourself in the position of "being a student." When you're in a position to learn from others, you'll put that knowledge to good use, even if "shutting down" is problematic.

September 24, 25, 26, 27
Libra, Cusp of Virgo

A quest for beauty, synthesis, and harmony animates people born in this birthday realm. Your Virgo flavor is fairly diluted, but still present. You are an analyzer but aren't as passionate (crazed and compulsive) about criticizing a situation as much as a true Virgo. Fortunately, Libra is a strong and seductive influence. I suspect you'll have the same love of beauty as Libras born later in the sign.

You could have a passion for analysis and more equilibrium than Libras animated by a "whatever" philosophy. Team playing and partnership is also an important aspect of this birthday zone. Look at authors F. Scott Fitzgerald (September 24) and William Faulkner (September 25). Their work was justly celebrated as summoning—and summing up—an entire world that's now vanished. They're still celebrated and are an important part of the English literature canon.

However, during their careers, they were assisted immeasurably by editor Maxwell Perkins, who helped them shape their books and worked with them over a period of many years. Alas, publishing nowadays doesn't foster the kind of editor/writer relationship authors enjoyed earlier in the twentieth century. So even if you don't have writing aspirations, be very aware that you'll function best with a partner, or partners. Yes, yes, yes—you'll be *fine* flying solo on projects and plans, and you'll also be more independent than Libras born later in the sign. However, you really do thrive on others' input to be at your best—and that's a good thing.

Author and dance critic Thea Singer is just over the border into Libra, with a September 24 birthday. "I cling voraciously to my Libraness," she explains. "I perceive the sign as being balanced and seeing both sides of things. I see Virgo as persnickety." Nevertheless, in a distinguished journalism career, which included frequent stints as a copy editor and proofreader, Singer admits that Virgo may have had an influence in her attention to detail. "I look more favorably on the Libra characteristics. I look at Virgo as negative—the parts of myself I have the most trouble with—for example, I can be very perfectionistic and concentrate on details—but it can make me tear my hair out," she laughs.

She had a dance career before turning to journalism, but came to dance late. "I started after college, at 21. Dancing helped bring out my Libra side—the balance, and the love of beauty. Becoming a dance critic is how these two signs are enmeshed with me. The aesthetic and spiritual side of it is the Libra side, but the writing about dance brings out my perfectionistic side." She sighs, "I labor over every word."

Singer recently had an opportunity to explore another topic—health and bioscience—in greater depth, in her new book *Stress Less*. In it, she interviewed a variety of Nobel prize–winning scientists and explored the world of "telemeres," the nerve endings that can indicate cell decay as we age.

"My goal was to represent the scientist's work accurately," she explains. "So I was very careful about the science writing in my book. I wanted to recognize nuances and subtleties rather than painting with a broad brush." It would have been easier to write a pop book about how exercise can lengthen your telemeres! People who are not like that can enjoy life more!

She does find her dominant Libra traits of balance decisive when assessing her personal relationships. "I don't like conflict and I have many, many good friends. I make good friends and keep them." Her friends range from old pals from high school to college friends to various work friends. "I'm not a group person," she says. "I like one on one relationships."

As our conversation draws to a close, she asks, "Do you think this is typical of Libra? I always have a contingency plan!" Even after a publisher requested she write a proposal focusing on telemeres (inspired by an article for O *Magazine*), she explains, "I immediately jumped back to teaching. I'm not comfortable seeing what will happen. I always have to have a safety net."

Final Thoughts

Since the next Libra cusp unites Venus with Pluto (now there's some drama!), Virgo-Libra's fusion of Mercury and Venus strikes me as harmonious, pleasant, and ripe with possibility for having an interesting life and lots of quirky and memorable friends. There's a built-in social ease that comes with lots of grace. You can be the center of a circle, and as long as you have a handle on the Libra dithering and the Virgo criticizing, this is a really lovely time to have a birthday.

Times of the year when you're "on fire" and should move all projects forward
May 17–24, September 20–27, November 19–26, January 18–25

Times of the year when you may feel compromised or that your judgment isn't as sound as you'd like
March 18–24, June 19–25, December 21–26

chapter nine

LIBRA-SCORPIO CUSP

The Signs at a Glance

Libra and Scorpio always remind me about the abduction of Persephone by Hades, and the mourning of Demeter, Persephone's mother. Here, Venus meets Pluto, and Pluto definitely is in a hostage-taking mode. The tension between these two signs can make for someone who can talk to anyone but doesn't always know what they're feeling. Or someone who wants to heal or cure others but has a few bad habits of their own.

Dates of Transition

Libra wraps up on October 22 or 23. Scorpio begins on October 24 or 25. If you're born October 22, you're definitely a

Libra. Those born October 25 are definitely Scorpio. The three days between can make for a super-powerful person, able to be with others and on their own. Or, this can be someone who feels bereft if they're not in a relationship, yet can't quite figure out how to be in one without thoroughly losing their own identity.

Details on the Cusp Aspects

Water and air (like Gemini and Cancer) can lighten up Scorpio, which is considered a "heavy" sign. Libra's direct nature gets complicated with Scorpio's strategic scheming, and the folks born in this cuspy zone can be happy working in classified jobs or have careers where information is shared on a need-to-know basis. The scales and the scorpion don't seem to have a lot in common. Astronomically, Libra is a very small constellation, while Scorpio spreads itself along the sky, and those who are just south of the northern latitudes will see the little stinger as two faint stars.

Libra wants to make friends, but not necessarily deeply, while Scorpio craves intimacy, but on their own terms. Sexy sensuality is a hallmark, and the best-adjusted individuals have an understanding of their appetites. These can be enormous! There's also a penchant for self-denial, since Scorpio has tremendous willpower and Libra craves direction. Pluto's rulership of Scorpio and Venus's rulership of Libra make for an unlikely partnership. Think of Persephone (Venusian) held hostage in the (Plutonic) underworld. Coping with depression or disappointments can be a lifelong theme and sometimes you say the opposite of what you feel. There is a depth that Libra doesn't usually have and a sensitivity that Scorpio doesn't usually manifest.

Personally, I find this cusp interesting because of the tension between Libra's equilibrium-seeking contrasts so vehemently with Scorpio's impulse for self-preservation and control. You may be someone as sweet as pie, but only fools will try to cross you more than once. I've seen people with this birthday ally themselves with partners they can totally manipulate. I've also seen the reverse. The important aspect of this birthday zone is that the inhabitants need to *feel* they are in control, whether they are or not. There are quirky positive aspects if you're born at this time. Use your Libra flexibility and versatility and your Scorpionic strategizing to get what you want! Libra-Scorpio are healthiest and happiest when they keep an open mind and surround themselves with lots of different people. There must also be a "helping others" component to your life. The Scorpio side can bring out your green thumb.

If you're born at the end of Libra, you'll be a more canny negotiator than a Libra born earlier. You also won't care if everyone is "happy" at the end of a negotiation session. Well, you will, but it won't be the overriding motivator.

If you're born at the start of Scorpio, you may miss out on Scorpio's "take no prisoners" penchant. You may also be plagued by self-doubt, particularly if parents were overbearing or controlling. Independence makes you happy, and finding the space between solitude and loneliness is your mission.

Lovers, Partners, Friends

Libra's Venus influence can make you attracted to people who have the right "look," but Pluto's influence on Scorpio means you could be attracted to those with destructive impulses. In my experience, Scorpios are highly skeptical, but having Libra so close can mute the suspiciousness in your nature. Is this a good thing? It can be, as long as you also work on being self-protective. Often, you can accept what you're told, instead of asking lots of questions. As with the Virgo-Libra, if this is your birthday, you may be more comfortable in a relationship where you let your partner to take the lead, particularly if you are with someone who wears their passions on their sleeve.

Libra-Scorpio bring a spirit of fairness to a relationship—at least you're willing to think about what's fair and equal. You also bring an ability to plan ahead. As long as you don't cling too dearly to Scorpio's "must maintain control at all costs" mindset—that's the recipe for getting blown away by infatuation! And that can leave you feeling at a disadvantage. But you know what? No one gets through life's rich pageant without a few nicks and scrapes. Scorpio is so well defended that occasionally the universe likes to see what happens when you have to improvise.

Fire signs (Aries, Leo, or Sagittarius) could be exciting but move too quickly. You need to know where you stand, and what's expected of you. Fire signs can keep others off balance, and they can also change direction much faster than you can. If you find this intriguing, that's great. I can pretty much guarantee a fire sign will bring a lot of activity and adventure to your life. You'll never know what's coming next. If you're with someone who's athletic or interested in social justice, your eyes can be opened.

You'd perceive earth signs (Taurus, Virgo, Capricorn) as consistent and calming. They'd be excellent business partners, and they'd also appreciate your consistency, reliability, and love of "the good life." Earth signs might be slow to warm up to you—and Scorpio's intensity can rub folks born under this element the wrong way. Also, these are people who may be more conservative than you. However, they can provide solace and stability if you're on the rebound from a volatile relationship.

Other air signs (Aquarius or Gemini) could be fun but frustrating. You'd be put in the position of always being responsible. Over time, you might feel some inequities with someone in the air category. If they are constantly canceling or changing plans, figure this is a pattern that will continue. This is an element that may work better as a colleague or platonic partner. But if they're fun and witty—they'll own you.

Water signs (Cancer, Scorpio, and Pisces) could be a fabulous fit. Sure, they're emotional. Yes, they have periods of shyness and awkwardness. But don't you just love them for it? And they would love you. They would identify and approve of parts of your nature you don't think anyone would notice, let alone appreciate.

Careers and Vocations
Libra-Scorpio

Actor, clergy, addiction counselor, bathroom tile specialist, credit counselor, engineer, funerary, insurance claims adjuster, hot air balloonist, jeweler, judge, journalist, music teacher, plumbing, sales and marketing, signmaker, spy, probate, sex worker, hair stylist, personal grooming consultant.

October 18, 19, 20, 21
Libra, Cusp of Scorpio

Wit and mystery come with this birthday. You have Libra's charm and Scorpio's ability to calculate. You love the idea of a "soul mate," but you can live happily independent (even though you can be funny and self-deprecating about your high standards). Leadership that has a well-tuned ear is one of the hallmarks of this birthday zone, and you can prompt huge loyalty from those around you. You can also make those around you a little bit crazy. French poet and visionary Arthur Rimbaud (October 20) was shot by lover Paul Verlaine.

Libra cusp of Scorpio people have a finger on the public's pulse. You know what appeals to others, and you also know you don't have to explore the "lowest common denominator." There's an eccentricity to your personality that may mystify some folks, but it can earn you lifelong fans. You have a desire for harmony, but you don't mind the chaos that comes before everything's in sync. You have a vivid imagination, and really need to be mindful of letting fantasy carry you away. Extremes are more comfortable for you than for other Libra folks, and you don't mind being controversial in your opinions.

There are some wonderful writers in this birthday neighborhood: playwright Wendy Wasserstein (October 18), John le Carré (October 19), and Carrie Fisher and Ursula K. Le Guin (October 21). Verbal expressiveness is a Libra trait, and the ability to see multiple perspectives is also one of your traits—some would say a gift. Wittiness is also something you value, particularly in a lover. You're drawn to folks because of how you communicate with them, not necessarily because of how you feel when you're with them.

You could be more sensitive than you think you are; that is, others who are rude or brusque might not bother you at first. And then, you could have that feeling of "sudden awakening," which has you saying, "Why is this person in my life?" It's not that you don't know your own mind or feelings; instead, I think what happens is that it's easy for you to just get on with things and then suddenly find you're really irked by carelessness.

Analysis is one of your greatest strengths and if you make the time to think through actions and consequences, comments and responses, you'll be successful. However, all the air signs are impulsive to some degree. Even though Scorpio is definitely breathing down your neck, the Libra nature will dominate.

And that nature comes with tremendous powers of persuasion. Wendy Wasserstein made a name for herself in the 1980s as a chronicler of neurotic (and funny) urban women navigating difficult families. She was constantly aiming to reveal the humanity in comedy, which is why her work has had such staying power. Though she died tragically young in her fifties, she exemplified Libra's friendly nature as a writer, and hopefulness as an air sign. Here's one of my favorite comments of hers (since taken up by legions of high school students for a yearbook quote): "Don't live down to expectations. Go out there and do something remarkable."

Libra's gift is that they can help others develop talent within themselves. I've known lots of Libra teachers and behind-the-scenes organizers. Your sign is skilled at knowing what others need to be at their best. You are armed with the judgment and courage of Scorpio, softened by Libra. Just be mindful so that you don't let people take advantage of your generosity and good nature.

However, if you do feel that others aren't respecting boundaries, or that they're breaking promises, or being dishonest, you'll take it to heart. You don't have Scorpio's skepticism about others and their motivations. You really want to believe the best in people, which is one reason why you have so many friends from many different walks of life!

October 22, 23
Libra-Scorpio Cusp

Scales or Scorpion? You get to be both. The Libra-Scorpio cusp is a maverick. You also have that Scorpion tendency of "taking no prisoners." But no matter how "out there" you get, self-protection and "being able to be in the bunker" are part of your survival arsenal. Like those born a few days before, you're able to function happily in a partnership. But you're essentially unknowable, which makes you fascinating to others. Your biggest danger is encountering those who wish to tame you.

I asked a friend, Pete G. (October 23), about being a Libra-Scorpio. He's had a long career in a variety of fields (engineering, information services), and he's got management skills, but he's also very skilled when cultivating clients or customers. He said:

> I remember that the strength of a Libra is in the way they can gently weigh both sides of an argument, and even argue both sides of an issue. In my occupation as a pre-sales support engineer, I would have to agree that this ability is a valuable tool that I use when I work with potential clients. By being able to "think like a client," I can identify where their motivations and hot buttons lie, and compare and contrast where the product I represent meets and assists their situation. However, a classically Scorpio characteristic is the venomous mean streak many Scorpios possess. I do find that when I am pushed, a lethal stinger exists!

Frankly, my experience with Libra-Scorpio is that you really hate using that stinger! You enjoy knowing you have it, but once it's deployed, you can revert back to your Libra self, and do some deep brooding over whether or not it was the right thing to do. If this chapter accomplishes anything, I hope you will take permission for having *and* using the stinger.

You also have determination and guts, and you can strike others as mysterious and unknowable, especially compared with other air signs. You are happy being independent—you don't "need" others the way Libra, Gemini, and Pisces do, and you really prefer having time to think, rather than responding immediately. Don't let others push you into a decision, but do listen to both sides—that open-mindedness is a strength for Libra and will do you well.

You can be in the spotlight, but in all likelihood, you don't need to have all the attention. Being a supporting player is satisfying, and much less pressure. You probably have Libra's gift for partnership.

Johnny Carson (October 23), was widely regarded as a cipher in his personal life, but his loyalty to producer Fred de Cordova, sidekick Ed McMahon, and band leader Doc Severinsen is unique in the history of television. Libra-Scorpio is skilled at being in a variety of alliances. You know what others need, and you know how to support without being imposing. As a result, you have the potential for excellent self-esteem—others should not be able to bulldoze you. And if they do, you can train yourself to resist!

I suspect that your life story has a lot of ups and downs. Others think you're more flexible, or easy-going, or persuadable than you are, and when they push you, they could find your normally genial manner changes. Still others (water signs Pisces and Cancer) may think you're more determined than you are. They may also think you need to do the close analysis of other folks, or are as fascinated with human nature as they are. My experience is that you are a trusting soul, and believe that what people show you is who they are. Looking for "hidden motivation" isn't really your style.

Ultimately, you can probably navigate a variety of careers (see chapter 14). You can build on a skill set that's very versatile. You're good with people and systems, a good judge of what's needed to complete a project, and flexible enough to know when a project needs to change. Deep down, you are a romantic, and you really want to believe the best of people.

October 24, 25, 26, 27
Scorpio, Cusp of Libra

Others think you're tough as nails, but Libra's Venus influence makes you a sucker for beauty. You probably have Scorpio's affinity for plants and growing green things. Others may think you don't need approval or corroboration. Your big secret? You do!

It's a lot easier for you to set limits and expectations for yourself than to have them for others. The best developed "on the edge" Scorpios respect others' independence and foster self-sufficiency in their children. And as much as you make what you do look easy, only you know exactly how much hard work, dedication, and determination go into what you love.

Kevin Kline (October 24), Hillary Clinton (October 26), and Sylvia Plath (October 27) are a trio of public figures who came into the public arena with obvious talent, yet who worked incredibly hard to develop their abilities to the highest point. Kevin Kline has happily played romantic leads and scurrilous villains in his career, a rarity for a film star, yet he always turns back to the stage, where he gets the excitement that comes with a live audience. Clinton continues to be faithful to her primary commitment to fairness for women and children. Sylvia Plath had a brilliant final few months as a genius poet, but what preceded was tireless hard work and dedication to the craft of writing.

If this is your birthday, you know how to keep a secret and how to play it safe. You are tremendously loyal—sometimes past the point of reason—and you always have a good reason for staying true to others. Pride is definitely a potential trouble spot, and you have more in common with Taurus and Leo than with Aquarius. Knowing when to stop a project, or let a relationship go, or move on from a job will be difficult because you are comfortable with consistency.

However, when you're feeling like you don't have choices, you need to read up on Libra, so you can access that part of your personality. Having Libra so close, yet not part of your Sun sign means you get to decide how you are going to foster and develop harmony in your life. Your partnerships will be as intense of those as Libra, but your inclination will be to stick with a partnership even if it ceases to work or be healthy or helpful to you.

You're a tough cookie, and it won't be long before you get a reputation for reliability and consistency in a workplace. (Yes, people will notice you.) In my experience those who have these birthdays are smart about self-analysis, yet not so strong about taking immediate, corrective action if a situation becomes difficult. You're excellent about jumping in on others' behalf, but not so quick to defend yourself. For recharging, you need extreme solitude (Scorpio) and garrulous gregariousness (Libra).

Interests could definitely include gardening (Scorpio), which could refresh your world-weariness. Plants won't talk back to you. Having a relaxing hobby (cooking, music, making art) is definitely recommended. Even if you don't have a hobby, you'll have a regular need for privacy, particularly when you feel others are "getting all up in your grill."

Your strengths include patience, strategy and willpower. Once you've set a course of action, there is absolutely no one who can deflect you. That said, there are times when you may think others are giving an opinion, or not supporting you when, in fact, you haven't given them enough information to have an opinion, and certainly haven't indicated you need support. One Achilles' heel is assuming others are as sensitive as you are—and think as deeply as you do. They aren't, and they're not. When you need help, you need to learn to ask for it. And, yes, this will sting!

Embrace the heroes and geniuses in this birthday neighborhood: Pablo Picasso (October 25), first environmentalist president Teddy Roosevelt and comedy genius John Cleese (both, October 26). These are excellent examples of the determination of a true path setter. When you question whether to stay or go, Libra's wishy-washy trait, think about the dedication Picasso had every time he picked up a paintbrush.

Final Thoughts

Personally, I love people born on this cusp. As a Libra myself, I understand their need for balance, harmony, humor, and doing good. However, I can relate to all the cusps because I also have a lot of Scorpio in my chart. I identify with your ability to scheme and plan for contingencies. At your best, you can win friends and influence people. At your least effective, you can't make up your mind, and you're somehow rude and distant to those who love you best. The Scorpion is a tough sign to have as a prominent influence, but it's excellent for making you tougher than you think you can be. Embrace the beauty, enjoy the plots, and grow a garden.

Times of the year when you're "on fire" and should move all projects forward

February 16–23, May 18–26, August 20–28, October 18–27, December 19–27

Times of the year when you may feel compromised or that your judgment isn't as sound as you'd like

January 17–25, April 16–24, July 19–27

chapter ten

SCORPIO-SAGITTARIUS CUSP

The Signs at a Glance

Secretive Scorpio meets let-it-all-hang-out Sagittarius in a cusp combination that can bring a sublime sense of humor. Scorpio-Sagittarius can criticize, calculate, comment, and then tell you how the world is going to receive the message. Pluto likes to work in the dark, but Jupiter prefers doing everything in public. Seriously—remember all those mighty feats of training the mortals and punishing them for hubris? Courageousness (that doesn't require applause) can be one of the wonderful by-products of this combination.

Dates of Transition

The Scorpion surrenders to The Archer on November 21 or 22. So those born before those dates (November 18, 19,

20) are Scorpio, cusp of Sagittarius. If you're born November 23 and afterwards, you're definitely a Sagittarius, with some Scorpion influence (lucky you!).

Details on the Cusp Aspects

As Scorpio is the most self-reliant, least emotionally "needy" water sign, the water influence here tends to be more perceptual and absorbent of others' feelings. I've found that, of all the fire signs, Sagittarius has the most consistent appetite for "fun," whether it's outdoor sports or random social assemblages, and is the least egotistical when it comes to getting strokes from others.

Jupiter's rulership of Sagittarius enhances your desire for fairness and justice. You can get very irked if you see an individual or a group of people getting cheated or exploited. And you'll need to take action, because Pluto's rulership of Scorpio increases your need to right any wrongs you see. You are much happier with revolution than gradual change, and you also have an anarchic side that can delight in chaos.

I think of Scorpio-Sagittairus as the "imaginative therapist" or the "worldly wise strategist." Others really shouldn't underestimate you, or think you are less serious than you are. Sometimes, you have a veneer of humor or dry wit, or above-and-beyond commitment to a cause. You're probably also highly social. Meeting new people, especially those who have top-level intelligence, can be an essential part of your career.

The Sagittarius influence can increase your athletic side, while Scorpio brings a precision to your life that most

Sagittarians would kill for (it's an accident- and gaffe-prone sign). To be fully "yourself" in the world, you'll need a cause (or two, or three) to spend energy on. You are generous, particularly with time and talents. Choose your charitable recipients carefully.

If you're born at the end of Scorpio, you probably don't have that full-on, dark, penetrating Scorpionic gaze, but you are graced with an ability to analyze. You also have a sense of humor that's more developed than other Scorpios. If you're lucky, you won't need to brood about life!

If you're born at the start of Sagittarius, you probably aren't chronically accident-prone as those born later in the sign. Your sense of humor that may be more subtle or difficult to classify, and you may also have a need for solitude that your fellow archers don't share. You'll be more skeptical about "pie in the sky" projects and you probably are less impulsive as well. Compulsive? Well, that Scorpio influence *can* bring out a little OCD!

Lovers, Partners, Friends

There's a lot of flexibility in whom you'd choose. You like intense and optimistic, adventurous and consistent. You have an open mind about loved ones. You love being a "fan" of your partner. Knowing you're with someone who loves what they do and who feels things deeply would be satisfying. Being with someone who knows how to leave you alone is also a good choice. But mostly, sharing your values is key. Vegans need to stick with vegans, and Pagans should stick with pagans. Less conflict!

You have a "caretaker" impulse for loved ones, and you definitely have a soft spot for those who need your energy, enthusiasm, encouragement, and ideas. As long as you don't find yourself in a situation where you're "in charge" of the other person (your sense of freedom would be tremendously compromised!), you bring a lot of really excellent qualities to a relationship.

So who's best for you? All the signs have good qualities, and those whom you'd enjoy would be Pisces-Taurus and Libra-Scorpio. Cancer-Leo (the other water-fire combo) might be sensitive, and easily bruised. You'd love their loyalty, but they could feel dependent in a way that's cloying.

Fire signs are always a good choice, but they would bring out your ability to "sizzle." Where you'd get along is in the realm of travel. You could plan adventures together and their curiosity would fuel yours. The Jupiter-Pluto combination makes you very conscious of the need to tear everything apart and start over. Since fire signs are initiators and doers (if not always finishers), you'd have lots in common philosophically.

Earth signs would be steady and reliable, but you may need to be the one who "takes charge." Earth signs will want to know what you think and feel, but they may not react or respond with the sensitivity you need. Unless they had a measure of water in their chart, you might not find the "depths" you need in a loved one.

Air signs would be charming and great for a short romance. You'd share a sense of humor and play. But if you're inconsistent and they're inconsistent, there may not be the staying power that a long-term relationship needs.

They have lots of ideas, however, and would be great as sounding boards for you. However, you may find the sedate and intense Scorpio side of your nature comes out more if they're the "fuss and fizz" types!

Water signs could meet you at your own level. There's a lot of passion in this sign, and since you have the Scorpio influence, you'd respond to how serious and respectful they are about intense feelings. Water signs will remind you of inconsistencies in your emotions, but they will also understand how that's a part of human nature and thoroughly forgivable.

Careers and Vocations
Scorpio-Sagittarius

Addiction counselor, adult care, archery and firearms, insurance claims adjuster and automotive insurance, animal care, automotive industry, bicyclist, blasting specialist, body piercing, golf, funerary (including cremation services), physical fitness trainer, heating and furnace work, plumber, probate tax law, tattoo artist, travel agent, veterinarian.

November 18, 19, 20
Scorpio, Cusp of Sagittarius

Yes, you're a Scorpio and yes, you have that Sagittarius influence. You're feistier than the typical Scorpio, and you're also willing to go public with a personal struggle, mission, or cause. Other Scorpios may strike you as neurotic and private, and they're likely to look at you as being more of a "loose cannon" than themselves. Nevertheless, your little corner of the zodiac has produced some visionaries, heroes, and martyrs, some of whom have departed this planet spectacularly (Lynryd Skynrd guitarist and co-founder Duane Allman, in 1971; Robert F. Kennedy, in 1968; all shared a November 20 birthday).

I love reflecting on the mutant genetic combo of these two creatures: the scorpion plus the centaur. What kind of critter are we talking about? Does the horse grow a stinger tail? Do you replace the bow and arrow with a pair of claws? Regardless of the physical form of this graft, Scorpio-Sagittarius has unique skills unmatched elsewhere in "cusp world." You think about how the world *should* work and you also have incredible planning and vision. If you're fortunate, you won't have Sagittarius's occasional gullibility and credulity. Thinking things through is always a strength. So is having a long memory. In my experience, only Capricorn and Virgo have the same ability to think sequentially and act logically. You like order, lists, and knowing where you stand.

You don't like to be pigeon-holed, and the worst thing someone can say to you is, "I know what you're like— you're one of those [fill in the blanks]." Unlike most true Scorpios, who revel in having a "secret" side, Sagittarius wants the freedom (and space) to reinvent themselves periodically. And, if you're lucky, you'll have an excellent sense of humor about this.

Scorpio's intensity lightens up for you folks. You have their sharp, critical ability, but you have a soft spot for humanity's foibles. You have huge sympathy and understanding for the oppressed and you can be easily prompted to take action. Scorpio is often content to plan and dispatch, but the Sagittarius influence makes you a doer, as well as unpredictable.

You love having a cause, and you're not shy about sharing your views. You can be a successful advocate for others, even if you don't always notice you could—and should—support yourself. I suspect you'll leave people "guessing" about you much of the time—wondering what you're "really like," wondering about gender preference, and then being surprised at whatever they learn about you!

And, as much as you'd like to control situations, or have the final say about the outcome, Sagittarius can give you a "get out of jail free card." Sagittarius can help you be less invested in minutiae, and more alert to the pleasures of improvisation.

Folks with your birthday can have technical expertise and gifts of logic and deduction (photography pioneer Louis Daguerre, November 18, and Cuban chess champion J. R. Capablanca, November 19). They can also have a love of exotic cultures, travel, and meeting new people (Alistair Cooke, Sir Samuel Cunard, founder of the famous shipping line, November 20). And you can also have a spiritual calling that requires great courage (Martin Luther, November 19), or loyalty to a group that pushes you into the political sphere (Wilma P. Mankiller, Cherokee activist).

Drive and guts will get you through. Insecurity isn't comfortable, and if you're feeling pushed, it's not a big deal for you to walk away. There are four fixed signs: Taurus, Leo, Scorpio, and Aquarius (the signs that come in the middle of a season). The latter two can deflect conflict by withdrawing from the fray. But that Sagittarius fire-sign energy can come to the fore and put you into a fight you didn't intend to participate in.

November 21, 22
Scorpio-Sagittarius Cusp

When media advisor and former reporter Dorie Clark was just twenty-six, she found herself advising presidential candidate Howard Dean as his New Hampshire campaign manager. She had wanted to make the jump from journalism to public policy and political activism full time, and the Dean opportunity opened numerous doors. Within months, she was asked to join Robert Reich's campaign. The former U.S. Labor Secretary under President Bill Clinton was running for governor of Massachusetts. Dorie's role was both as press liaison and advisor, and earned her kudos from the candidate. "My campaign benefited tremendously from Dorie Clark's communications acumen, relationships with the press, and instinctual grasp of quick-moving political developments," he commented. "She is a respected strategic thinker, a proven press liaison, and someone who can drive positive media coverage."

With a November 22 birthday, Dorie is zero degrees of Sagittarius. So she is an official Archer, but just barely. The investigative aspects of her professional activities— especially anticipating arguments and political brinksmanship—are unquestionably a Scorpio trait. Yet her straightforward methodology for guiding political candidates and causes into the clear light of day speaks to the Sagittarius influence. "I definitely have some of the passion of Scorpio," she admits. "I'm intense about certain topics, and no one would say I'm unmoved by life."

Still, she feels her Sagittarius Sun makes the crucial difference. "My understanding of the sign is that they're philosophical. My perception of Scorpio is that they're supposed to be a little manipulative, and overly ambitious and intense in a self-serving or solipsistic way," she says, and adds with a laugh, "I tell myself I'm not like that!"

Competitiveness can definitely be an attribute. Here are some memorable athletes born on November 22: Billie Jean King and Boris Becker (the youngest Wimbledon winner). In their prime each was quick and decisive on the court. Also born on that day is Sir Peter Hall, London director-producer whose years at the National revolutionized that theater. Hall is an interesting case, because he is also a significant opera director. His emphasis on the National Theater's programs, reflecting theatrical traditions across Europe all the way to the Far East, was revolutionary.

Though you understand the importance of "sticking to things," the Sagittarius influence helps you "ease on down the road" as needed. The Sagittarius influence also gives you a quirky worldview that others will find magnetic and compelling. You're popular without really working at it, because folks like the way you think and the way you communicate. And though you may have healthy self-esteem, unless there are other factors in play, you won't thrive on approval the way some other folks do. Your independence will be highly attractive to others. Some may be intimidated by your confidence and breezy know-how. If that's the case, learn to recognize the signs: folks saying, "Oh, you're so much better than me, can you do it?" so you don't end up being responsible for projects or activities that really are the purlieu of another person.

Finally, here's a quirky trait: Are you accident-prone? Sagittarius can be an amazing athlete, but I've known plenty of Sagittarians who are always sporting a scratch or bruise. Since Sagittarius rules the hips, mishaps may come from bumping open a closed door. I've driven with Sagittarians and Sagittarius-Capricorn folks, and they can make a country lane seem like the Autobahn!

November 23, 24, 25, 26
Sagittarius, Cusp of Scorpio

Sagittarius folks can be accident-prone, but with Scorpio so near to your Sun sign, you're probably more sure footed than other Archers. You'll have Sagittarius traits, like an interest in exotic cultures, and possibly a wanderlust. But you like to plan your trips carefully, and you're happy as an "armchair traveler" as well. Personal transformation and innovation is your guiding light, and you also have a good grasp on "what the public wants."

My personal favorite Marx brother, Harpo (November 23), makes an excellent guiding spirit for you. Born Adolph Marx, he was the second oldest Marx brother and a classic middle child between Leonard (Chico) and Julius (Groucho). His memoir, *Harpo Speaks,* is one of the most charming and beguiling documents about showbiz. As you might expect, Harpo has an exquisite sense of absurdity. He also is thoroughly lacking in ego, which makes his book unique among movie stars. I thought this extract sums up the Sagittarius sense of humor and love of sports:

> You can always spot a guy who grew up poor on the East Side by watching him go for a swim. When he gets in a pool he will automatically start off with a shallow kind of breast stroke, as if he were pushing away some invisible, floating object. This was a stroke you had to use when you jumped in the East River. It was the only way you could keep the sewage and garbage out of your face.

If one of these dates is your birthday, salvation comes when you can laugh at yourself. You can collaborate with others, so you probably have a broader vision of the world. Innovation is also a trait: consider American composers Scott Joplin (November 24) and Virgil Thompson (November 25). Their music still sounds modern to our ears.

You can also develop a taste for luxury or indulgence, or romantic fantasy taken to an extreme. Dwarf Parisian painter Henri de Toulouse-Lautrec (November 24) looked at the working girls of Paris as princesses in castles, even though he famously said: "I paint things as they are. I don't comment. I record." (Yes, a touch of nearsightedness helps you overlook the flaws!) So is sincerity—Lautrec really loved the girls of the *demimonde* (class of women thought to be of doubtful morality), commenting: "A professional model is like a stuffed owl. These girls are alive."

In short, your sign is drawn toward vitality and excitement. The limelight may not be a comfortable spot to work in, but working near it, or just on the edges, would be agreeable. With Scorpio as an influence, be aware that it will be normal for you to have periodic anxiety, or even paranoia (especially about the motivations of others). And you also have a secret side. As a result, you may spend more time than you need to explaining how honest and up front you are with others. You will expect sincerity in turn, no matter how unlikely or unjustified. And the best way you can get over that disappointment is to keep a sense of humor.

Back in the 1950s, when he started drawing his daily comic strip, "Peanuts," Charles Schulz (November 26) was a revolutionary. Hitherto, comics had been slapstick or vaudeville in their nature with broad humor, easy stereotypes, and silly situations. Schulz wrote about kids as kids, and found a true spirit of childhood in Charlie Brown, Lucy and Linus, Schroeder and Violet, Snoopy and Woodstock. So what if they occasionally sounded like graduate students in psychology! Schulz's characters are intense and eccentric, adventurous and consistent—just like Scorpio-Sagittarius. Seriously, don't you wish you had some of Snoopy's style?

Final Thoughts

This is a very cool time to have a birthday. You can be as complex and interesting as a Scorpio, with a measure of lightness and sweetness alongside. Having childlike wonder at all the crazy things in this world is part of the nature of your cusp. But you must have enough self-knowledge so that you can handle disappointments, even when they're unexpected. This cusp can easily be embittered or feel cheated when there are bumps in the road. Try not to be too trusting, and remember that one of your purposes on earth is to improve the lot of those less fortunate (which can including making sure "justice is done").

Times of the year when you're "on fire" and should move all projects forward

January 18–24, March 17–24, July 20–27, August 18–27, November 17–24

Times of the year when you may feel compromised or that your judgment isn't as sound as you'd like

February 15–23, May 18–25, August 18–25

chapter eleven

SAGITTARIUS-CAPRICORN CUSP

The Signs at a Glance

Sagittarius and Capricorn combine two very powerful forces in the universe: generosity and limit-setting, short-term satisfaction and long-term gains. And yes, that does sound like a mutual fund, which is the sort of investment both signs would approve of, as long as there was some social justice built in. Jupiter and Saturn aren't the best of friends in the canon of Greek mythology, and how they unite here always makes for a distinctive, strong-willed personality.

Dates of Transition

Sagittarius ends on December 21 or 22. Capricorn begins on December 22 or 23. Those of you born December 20, which is the Winter Solstice, are Sagittarius, and those born December 23 are Capricorn. No matter what birthday you have, unless you have incredibly thoughtful family members, you'll have a combo "birthday-Christmas" present every year.

Details on the Cusp Aspects

Fire and earth are primal. Fire is about consumption, and earth is all about acquisition. Sagittarius can bring an athletic ability, and Capricorn enhances endurance and practice. The Archer meets The Goat, and each tries to make the other laugh. Sagittarius is inherently positive and jovial, as befits its rulership by Jupiter. Capricorn can be dour or "expecting the worst" (okay, they call it being realistic). That's what happens when Saturn runs the show.

Here's how I see these planets: Jupiter is like the generous uncle, who brings you the latest trendy toy for your birthday, makes everyone laugh and connect with one another at your party, but has someplace else to go before the clean-up (busy Jupiter, making everyone happy!). Saturn is like the miserly uncle, who slips into your party after the festivities have started and gives you an "appropriate" present: a savings bond that will mature in twenty-five years. Saturn's comments are usually apt, but hardly merry, yet Saturn stays late to help with the clean-up. He's a little grim, but the old boy does make sense.

So these are the two influences on your Sun sign. Are you divided by them, torn between their stories? That is your situation in a nutshell. The happiest Sagittarius-Capricorns I know find work that has unpredictability built in. Sagittarius can improvise, and Capricorn is respectful of limits, techniques, and boundaries. Some Sagittarius-Capricorns have a droll or ironic affect, so others around them don't always know when they're joking. Your sense of humor is definitely more "fringe" than mainstream, especially as you get older.

If you're born at the end of Sagittarius, you'll be more serious and more prone to self-analysis that the typical Sagittarius. You'll also be harder on yourself. Whereas most Sagittarius folks can shrug off a personal failure or imploded project, you can brood, and play the "what if" game. Your advantage is Capricorn influence, which makes you learn from your mistakes!

If you're born at the beginning of Capricorn, you'll be lighter than the typical Capricorn, and also more capable of working with groups of people. Either way, you'll have leadership abilities, and the vision to get others excited about your projects. You can be responsible with finances for a group project but not always so mindful about your own needs and means.

Lovers, Partners, Friends

Your own sign would be easy to relate to—you have temperamental affinities, plus an enjoyment of getting things done, or getting moving. You'd enjoy Aquarius-Pisces, Leo-Virgo (as long as they didn't fuss), and Aries-Taurus (they'd get you organized).

You would share a sense of humor and wanting to make a difference in the world with other fire signs. You would also share passion, which means your argumentative side could be constantly provoked. Now, some fire and earth folks *like* this sensation, and even thrive on tension. If you end up with someone who finds fault with trifles at a restaurant, think twice.

Earth signs (Taurus, Virgo, and Capricorn) would be consistent and reliable, and could help you relax. They could also, by their own consistencies, make you feel bold and adventurous. No matter how much of a couch potato you are in your head, there are some earth signs who would treat you as if you were Douglas Fairbanks as Robin Hood, leaping over the ramparts every day.

Air signs (Gemini, Libra, and Aquarius) would amuse you. You'd certainly never be bored. But would you know where they are all the time? Would their innate changeability and need to reverse direction make you nervous, and also less reliable? You would find them fun, but you might also find they have moved on, just when you started feeling like you were getting to know them. Make sure you can count on them.

Water signs (Cancer, Scorpio, and Pisces) would be fascinated—and occasionally appalled—by some of your choices. Sagittarius-Capricorn does come with some materialism, especially if you can get your hands on the latest electronic toy or sporting equipment. Water signs like to connect emotionally, and you might have this feeling: "You think I'm deeper and more complicated than I am!" However, water signs would be tremendously supportive, particularly when you get into trouble and are very loyal. As long as you don't mind feeling like "the kid" in the relationship, there's great joy to be had here.

Careers and Vocations
Sagittarius-Capricorn

Accounting, animal care (including wildlife), antiques (dealing, restoration), archery, architecture, asphalt (paving and related fields), automotive, bail and other bond services, baseball batting cage owner, bathroom tile specialist, bicyclist, body piercing, chiropractor, concrete-cement, contracting, environmental fields, financial institutions, fence building, golf, heating and furnace work, investment specialist, mason/brickwork, physical fitness trainer, property management, tattoo artist, travel agent, veterinarian.

December 17, 18, 19, 20
Sagittarius, Cusp of Capricorn

You are definitely a Sagittarius, but that Capricorn influence is stabilizing, *and* it gives you a method for your madness (when you need it!). This birthday comes with a dash of rebellion and a determination that puts you apart from other Sagittarius folks. Capricorn's influence gives you tenacity and the ability to simplify. Capricorn will bring you back to basics, again and again. Consider Keith Richards (December 18), stalwart buccaneer guitarist for the Rolling Stones. No matter what musical flavors were afoot in the Stones' decades-long career, it was Keith's signature blues-inflected guitar playing that cut through every other trend Mick Jagger wanted to impose.

If your birthday comes now, you have a flair that few can match and an appetite for risk taking that's irresistible to others. Sagittarius-Capricorn folks love to see a long and complicated project right to the bitter end. And they also have a sense of humor and coping mechanisms that Capricorns later in the sign wouldn't have. Other Sagittarius cusp of Capricorns in the arts include filmmaker Stephen Spielberg (December 18), groundbreaking actress Cicely Tyson (December 19), and quirky long-lived British film star/actor Sir Ralph Richardson.

Like Libra, you have an inherent "on the one hand, on the other hand" duality in your nature. You also have a taste for doing things "the hard way." The worst thing a partner can do to you is rush you along—whether it's selecting a meal, or deciding on a house. Like all the Sagittarians and Capricorns, you have a fondness for travel. The prospect of gathering camping gear and setting off for parts unknown can be stressful, but ultimately exciting. You will strike some folks (the conservatives and the emotionally delicate) as being bold and determined. Even if you haven't made up your mind, you bring a confidence that makes others take notice.

Because you combine Jupiter and Saturn as influences, and for you, Jupiter is still dominant, you could get into a bad habit: second-guessing your own needs and desires. Realism comes second to the dream. Fortunately, you are a sign with enormous reserves of good luck—Jupiter loves to reward risk takers!

In my experience, Sagittarius cusp of Capricorn people are curious about others and can be very indulgent when it comes to dealing with or being attracted to quirky, challenging, or even argumentative personalities. A spirit of forgiveness is one of your strengths—a willingness to over-look the poor choices others make is one of your deficits.

When you feel "things aren't going your way" as you'd like them to, consider reading up about Capricorn. They have a lot of difficulties in their lives—many of their own making—but they are reliable, dependable, and very inde-pendent.

December 21, 22
Sagittarius-Capricorn Cusp

Skating on a thin edge—you're either a Sagittarius or Capricorn, depending on the year. This is also the time of the Winter Solstice, and it's helpful to remember that the traditional holiday of Saturnalia is all about turning roles topsy-turvy and indulging in revelry that mocks traditional roles. If you're in this birthday neighborhood, you'll have sympathy for the underdog—and a nose for underdogs!

Giacomo Puccini, opera composer, did something revo-lutionary with the denizens of *la vie boheme* ("long live Bo-hemian life!") by creating one of the most beloved operas: *La Boheme*. This was also revolutionary because Puccini identified and defined a new class: the underclass devoted to creating art. (You might be more familiar with the story of *La Boheme* in its modern incarnation, Broadway hit *Rent*.) Here's another musician who took the hippie freak show someplace dark and gnarly: Frank Zappa (December 21). Zappa was in a rare category: a genius who could also work with groups of people. His witty cynicism about hippie cul-ture referenced modernist composers and twelve-tone scales. His music appealed to middle school kids because of the "potty" humor, but also to aesthetes, because of his arcane references.

The people I know with these birthdays are independent and uncompromising. The deal with Capricorns is that they're old when they're young and young when they're old. Sagittarius, however, can stay youthful and responsive as long as there is some adventure, travel, and exercise in their life (particularly that which works out the upper thigh, Sagittarius's part of the body). It's hard to believe now that broadcaster Diane Sawyer (December 22) began her career as an aide to Richard Nixon. Her ability to take her job seriously and herself less seriously has only improved through the years. She and Barbara Walters (another cuspy person) have had careers in a difficult medium for decades.

Tim D'Onfro of Cambridge, Massachusetts, has a December 21 birthday. He is a true Sagittarius, right down to his philosophy major at Boston University. "I associate Sagittarius with being both physical and intuitive," he explains. "I'm interested in all religions and philosophies, mostly the Eastern Asian, but also Greek philosophy and the work of people like Jean-Paul Sartre." For Tim, studying and immersing himself in a variety of belief systems is deeply rewarding. "I like the idea of having as wide a perspective as I can, and getting as much wisdom as I can so I have a full perspective on what's going on in the world. I want to strive to be the best person I can be and learn a lot about how other people think and see things from their perspective," he says.

In his childhood, he played soccer, a sport I think of as being highly Sagittarian (which rules the hips and upper thigh). In high school and college, he was a serious skiier and also enjoys skateboarding. Living in Cambridge, adjacent to Boston, he uses his bicycle for transportation as much as he can.

As I spoke to him, I heard definite Capricorn traits coming out. He sometimes has difficulty with focus and dealing with distractions so he has developed coping strategies for follow-through. "I'm not so organized, and I'm not always sure what I'm going to do," he explains.

"I have to be really organized and structured in what I do," he says. "I've gotten really good at doing what I need to do to keep myself on track." As he enters his early thirties, he has decided to return to school, and pursue a truly Capricorn field of study: IT and computer science.

In my experience, I've found the cardinal signs, those that begin the four seasons—Aries, Cancer, Libra, and Capricorn—will definitely exert an influence on their adjoining signs. Capricorn can be a grounding influence, and it can also increase the Sagittarius-Capricorn person's ability to stick to a schedule, a plan, or a complicated sequence of actions.

December 23, 24, 25, 26
Capricorn, Cusp of Sagittarius

Resilience and defiance characterize these early Capricorns. Some have late-in-life success, like writer Quentin Crisp (December 25). Some have intense organizational skills and visionary leadership abilities, like the first

Church of Jesus Christ of Latter-Day Saint, Joseph Smith (also December 25). Some figure out how to see what others can't see, and then show them what's there, like revolutionary Renaissance astronomer Tycho Brahe (December 24). If you're born in this part of the zodiac, you're a Capricorn. You do have the potential to be steady and dependable. But you also have Sagittarius's wildness and tendency to bite off more than you can chew.

Having a wild streak may make you naturally seductive, like Ava Gardner (December 24). I sympathize with anyone who tries to tell you "Slow down!" This cusp, like the two already mentioned, will bring you personal courage. You have Sagittarius's need for justice and resolution, and you also have Capricorn's gut-level knowledge that life isn't supposed to be easy. You know that bumps in the road are features of the road, rather than impossible obstructions. You don't mind saying things that shock others—you might be interested in alternative cultural byways (tattoos, body piercing, extreme sports). You also have a slightly bemused perspective that makes you a visionary. Having the vision *and* the strength to carry it through is a rare and special gift!

Are you interested in having your own business? Or are you curious about working in travel, education, or banking industries? You have Capricorn's toughness without the doom-and-gloom. You have focus, without Sagittarius's tendency to be diffuse. You also have a sense of humor and an understanding of the vagaries of human nature. In short, unless there are other aspects present in your chart that bring out the misanthropic side—Lady Fortune is happy to smile upon you.

I've known Sagittarius-Capricorn folks who have multiple careers—which somehow coexist brilliantly. Matthew Arnold (December 24) is remembered mostly as a poet. But during his lifetime, he worked full time as an inspector of schools in Great Britain (education is a Sagittarius interest; budgets and structures are Capricorn). Arnold's best-known poem, "Dover Beach," is still one of the greatest verse epics on the dissolution of emotional intimacy.

Final Thoughts

If this is your birthday zone, you need to understand that you will periodically need to rebel, and that rebellion may be followed by a period of time working very hard at a solitary interest. Wanting to change the world and knowing how to break down a project into small and manageable steps are great gifts from the gods. One of your challenges may be deciding exactly what it is you're "supposed" to do for work. My view of your sign is that you can "do it all."

Times of the year when you're "on fire" and should move all projects forward

February 17–24, April 17–24, August 21–27, October 18–24, December 18–26

Times of the year when you may feel compromised or that your judgment isn't as sound as you'd like

March 18–24, September 20–26, June 18–24

chapter twelve

CAPRICORN-AQUARIUS CUSP

The Signs at a Glance

Capricorn's Eeyore-like gloom meets with Piglet's spirited sense of play in Capricorn-Aquarius. Looking back and looking ahead all at once is an impossible feat for most of us; although, it seems as if Capricorn-Aquarius folks have eyes in the back of their heads. Saturn, which says, "Here's how it should be," and Uranus, which says, "There's more going on than you think," combine in a visionary way. You can learn a lot from Capricorn-Aquarius people, and I absolutely guarantee they will not be vain about any of their great gifts.

Dates of Transition

Capricorn eases into Aquarius on January 20 or 21, depending on the year. So if you're born January 18 or 19, you'll get some Aquarian influence. And if you're born January 22, or a few days after, you'll be a more-responsible-than-usual Water Bearer. Those born on January 20 or 21 will feel torn between their need to take charge and their desire to abdicate control. Creativity can mix with strong discipline to produce someone who's technically adept at an artistic pursuit, or who has a creative flair when it comes to figuring out structures.

Details on the Cusp Aspects

Earth and air don't always have a lot to say to one another. Earth likes consistency, while air needs change. Earth enjoys doing the same things in the same way, while air constantly needs to change it up. And for my money, Aquarius is the most adventurous air sign, and probably the most adventurous sign of all, while Capricorn is the most grounded, consistent, and routine-loving. Capricorn's Saturn rulership craves limits, gravitates towards responsibility, and "expects the worst" at times. Aquarius's Uranian rulership says, "What if" about darn near everything! At your best, you'll be an improviser who knows what's next on the road. At your most disadvantaged, you'll stop yourself before you start, and lose interest in projects or people long before you've given them a chance.

Capricorn tends to take on projects that they can fly solo on. It's a sign that doesn't need others to assist them, or even acknowledge the work. Aquarius also has distinct ideas on how a project should go, but they are very open-minded about hearing alternatives. However, this sign reserves the right to change course abruptly the moment you think they've committed to a course of action! I've seen—more than a few times, by the way—people who are inscrutable to others, but have great ideas. These people might prefer not to be the leader, however, since it means others will rely on them. And that makes for pressure!

The deeper we move into January, the more Capricorn has the capacity to change. Earthy rigidity starts to loosen up. So there's some breathing room for those born closer to the sign of the water carrier. Creativity and a freewheeling sense of possibility replace the "we need to do it this way because we do it this way" philosophy of the goat. Dependability mixed with a need for freedom comes with these birthdays. There can also be a pleasant and humorous personality. Capricorn tends to take things very seriously, while full-on Aquarians are so "above the fray" that you are left wondering, well, what *do* they feel.

If you're born at the end of Capricorn, you're a solid citizen with a tendency to resist being pigeon-holed. You're ambitious and have some wild ideas. You also have less tolerance for routine and predictability (Capricorn is fascinated by systems and structure, and is comfortable doing things "the same way" and at their pace).

If you're born at the start of Aquarius you have leadership ability, but you're not always aware of the need of followers (you're a fairly powerful personality, so looking behind you is not a typical response). You don't mind being a little erratic, though you find unpredictability untenable in others. Leadership abilities come with this birthday, as does creativity.

Lovers, Partners, Friends

Independent and proud, your sign can go long periods between relationships. Friendship is important, but you don't crave the zing of passion that air and water signs love so much, and that can make life interesting and unpredictable. That airy influence makes for compatibility with many elements. But I think you'd be most comfortable with Scorpio-Sagittarius and Pisces-Taurus. Virgo-Libra might also appeal to you.

Back in the 1990s, the term "codependency" was a buzzword in therapeutic circles. What it meant was that some people have that "urge to merge," so that they develop unhealthy dependency on their partner. Instead of spreading out normal and healthy human needs among the community, one person takes it all.

Now, in my experience, I haven't found a lot of Capricorn-Aquarius people who have that "urge to merge." However, I have found some Capricorn-Aquarius people who *attract* those with that particular need. It might be part of your life's journey to spend time with another person who depends on you, and who makes you the center of your life. Yes, you will find this suffocating. But not right away. Recognizing that this is happening takes some time. Just be aware that you project conflicting traits: independence and spontaneity, consistency and openness.

Fire signs (Aries, Leo, and Sagittarius) would be lots of fun, and you could definitely build a life together. However, their enthusiasm and short-term intensity could leave you breathless, and confused. "What do they really want?" is a question that could quickly be followed by "I am really very tired!"

Air signs (Gemini, Libra, and Aquarius) would help you access the more buoyant side of your nature. They also would keep you from brooding too much. Any of these signs would be fun, as long as you'd be willing to be the final decision maker. Air signs tend to be chameleonic, so the more "Aquarian" you are, the more "airey" they are! The Capricorn side of your nature craves consistency. That's not always in the air-sign wheelhouse.

Earth signs (Taurus, Virgo, and Capricorn) would definitely relate to your practical side, your love of material comfort, and—what's that? You don't have a love of material comfort? Sure you do! Maybe not to the extent of a Taurus, but wouldn't it be fun to spend time with people who have a real work ethic and don't always want to go play?

Water signs (Cancer, Scorpio, and Pisces) could be reassuring and loving. They would remind you that it's important to know what you are feeling. They would also have enough fun that you would partake of different kinds of entertainment, travel, and food when you're with them. Water signs have sensitivity, but they would also be able to leave you alone, when that's what you want.

Careers and Vocations
Capricorn-Aquarius

Accounting, air conditioning, airlines, alternative health care, apartment management, animal care (including wildlife), antiques (dealing, restoration), archery, architecture, asphalt (paving and related fields), auctions, automotive, bail and other bond services, baseball batting cage owner, bathroom tile specialist, bicyclist, body piercing, chemist, chiropractor, computers, concrete-cement, contracting, environmental fields, costumer, electrician or electrical field, financial institutions, fence building, golf, guidance or career counseling, heating and furnace work, investment specialist, mason/brickwork, physical fitness trainer, property management, radio engineer, radiology refrigeration technology, tattoo artist, travel agent, veterinarian.

January 15, 16, 17, 18
Capricorn, Cusp of Aquarius

Capricorn's heaviness eases up with these birthdays. Yes, you're a Capricorn, but so close to Aquarius that "lightening up" comes easily. You're a "plugger," but distractible. You may find completing tasks much more difficult unless there's a hard and fast deadline. Your sense of humor is your saving grace, and you probably have a vivid and unusual imagination. Finding the humor in situations that devastate others is definitely a deficit at times. You may find that you've moved on while others may need more time to process or consider a situation.

This makes you a good leader, and someone who can wear a variety of hats. Capricorn can be skilled at handling a budget, while Aquarius can see the big picture and what direction to go. If you are able to reconcile the conservative and rebellious sides of your nature, you can have a very interesting career. You might also need to have a variety of jobs, and experiment with everything from business to human services, to communication and education, to science. You have air-sign curiosity and earth-sign logic. This is powerful but can occasionally send you adrift. Which direction should you go? Consider a winding path, rather than a straight shot to the top. You have to accommodate your love (and need) for novelty when you are choosing your career. You also need to be in a career that has change and opportunities for growth within it.

A. A. Milne (January 18), Winnie the Pooh's creator, had a parallel career as a playwright of frothy comedies of manners like Mr. Pim Passes By. Earlier in the twentieth century, it was easier for writers, particularly British ones, to have publishing careers in a variety of venues. Take encouragement from his career and reserve the right to be serious or whimsical. You have a huge capacity for hard work. You have a huge capacity for playing. Saturn's seriousness and hermit tendencies gets a big jolt of vitamins from Uranus's need for change, tendency to bring excitement, and ability to gather the troops.

These are personality traits to revel in. Isn't it a kick to feel like you can loosen up? Isn't it better to have some breathing room, and an ability to interact with others? Yes, you take risks with creativity, but a freewheeling sense of possibility is a healthy replacement for the "we need to do it this way because we do it this way" philosophy of the goat. Of course, you can still be dependable, and your need for freedom will keep your life interesting. And, you will not have the "dour aspect" of many Capricorns—I've known lots of folks in this birthday zone with a pleasant and humorous personality. Capricorn tends to take things very seriously, while full-on Aquarians are so "above the fray" that you are left wondering, well, what *do* they feel.

Trust me, having a certain amount of "cool," can be highly attractive to others, and excellent self-protection. Musician Gene Krupa (January 15), novelist William Kennedy (January 16), hair-mogel empire-builder Vidal Sassoon (January 17), and suave-beyond-measure Cary Grant (January 18) were born in this zone of the zodiac. And if you want visionaries, Martin Luther King (January 15) and Benjamin Franklin (January 17) changed the world in which they lived. Both were physically brave individuals, but their conviction mostly shone through their use of the language, which was graceful, forceful, and memorable. These two definitely have some of the "magic" you'll find when Capricorn and Aquarius collaborate!

January 19, 20
Capricorn-Aquarius Cusp

You could be either Capricorn or Aquarius with this birthday, and a certain amount of personal confusion definitely comes with this natal day. Let's start with January 19, and a pair of spectacularly self-destructive visionary artists: Edgar Allan Poe and Janis Joplin. The Aquarius-Capricorn blend in their charts made them extraordinarily productive. They were also notable for their enormous appetites for transformative experiences. Both of these artists took something old-fashioned and gave it a modern twist. Poe took the eighteenth century genre of "gothic" novel, added suspense, which virtually didn't exist in literature hitherto, and created horror. His characters are all victims of their appetites and their manias—whether of hubris or circumstance.

Joplin took country blues and hard rock rhythms, and cranked the fusion through a stack of Marshall amps, changing the role of women in rock and roll forever. She could take a rock song and make it plaintive, and she could take a folk song and rip out the jams. She was an extraordinary artist and a visionary. You listen to Joplin's voice and think she's a thousand years old, not in her twenties. Both of these artists are useful examples of the magic-making that occurs in this birthday zone. Your challenge will be (a) living up to it, and (b) not being destroyed by it.

You probably have a strong desire to move from project to project or person to person. Others may define you as "fickle," but your self-preservation (mental and otherwise) comes from being able to recognize when something is not working, pick up your pieces and move on. Ultimately, this is a strength, and it will serve you well, especially if you end up in a position of leadership—where you have to make quick decisions, process, and move on.

Take Italian nouveau vague filmmaker Federico Fellini (January 20). During his career he had a consistent and recognizable surrealist style along with an unpredictability.

When he was making movies in the 1950s and 1960s, film fanatics couldn't wait to see where his imagination would go next. Fellini has a birthday twin colleague in later filmmaker David Lynch (*Blue Velvet, Twin Peaks*). The film work of both men is notable for its eccentric characters and fascination with freakishness. Not to say everyone with this birthday shares this characteristic, but there's a deep-sourced curiosity not shared by most.

One of my favorite astronauts is the great Buzz Aldrin (January 20). Recently, he published his memoirs: *Magnificent Desolation: The Long Journey Home from the Moon*. Aldrin has been a very active spokesperson for NASA and a phenomenal ambassador for the space program, and these memoirs really are extraordinary. I have read the chapter that concerned the actual landing of the Apollo 11 module many times to children, because Aldrin sums up the senses of what it feels like to be in the group that first landed on the Moon. His description of walking on the surface of the Moon—the slight give under his boots and the view of the shades of gray in the craters and rocks—is poetic and evocative. Later in the book, he talks about his personal journey and difficulties, including recovery from substance abuse. He's honest, straightforward, and eternally optimistic—Aldrin is a glorious role model.

So if you're drawn to extremes and testing yourself, you're in tune with this birthday. If you want to change the world and have a ball while you do it, you thoroughly understand the nature of Capricorn-Aquarius. And if you find that your take on things is a little different from those in the mainstream, or that you're a few steps ahead (and no one is noticing yet), enjoy the advantage. We look to The Goats doing the do-si-do with the Water Bearer to show us where to go, and how to get there.

January 21, 22, 23, 24
Aquarius, Cusp of Capricorn

Gracefully competitive, Aquarius makes you an idealist, but you can never walk away from practical concerns. You are not an emotional softie, and you get bored unless there's a certain amount of competitiveness. Humphrey Bogart (January 23) famously began his performing career as the adorable baby drawn by his artist mother, Maud Bogart. His stage career was short-lived and reviews of the period talk about how stiff and dull he is. However, a few years under his belt, a lip injury that caused him to lisp, and a move to Hollywood helped him find his rightful place as a morally compromised gangster type with more ambiguity and mystery.

Theater director Jeff Mosser (formerly of the Humana Festival of the Actors' Theatre of Louisville) is a just-over-the-line Aquarian (January 22). For him, the Capricorn influence on his Aquarian Sun is enjoyable, and even calming. "My brain needs to be active and engaged and processing during the day," he says. "But if I'm going to direct a play, I have to do some math later that afternoon." In his life, Aquarius exerts a social influence. "The Aquarius in me needs to be engaged in discussions with other people. The Capricorn needs to process and work at my own pace." Since both signs tend to be highly independent, Mosser's career choice of theater arts combines an ability to supervise others, create curricula for education programs, and think about the small details of performance.

Self-sufficiency is one hallmark of both Capricorn and Aquarius. Oh, and do you have a tendency to dramatize? You have excellent communication skills, particularly when it comes to explaining difficult concepts. You will always resist a family dynamic that's "too confining." The freedom that Aquarius needs matched with the steady pre-dictability that makes Capricorn comfortable can make for some awkward interludes growing up. You may surprise yourself by what you need to rebel against!

You are probably mindful of trends. Even if you don't follow them, you can recognize what "the next big thing" is going to be. This can put you into an interesting rela-tionship with a group—you may need to be the person who reminds us all that vision is important to success. You also have a craving for freedom, and, like the Capricorn cusp of Aquarius folks, your life will include many career paths. You can get along with young and old, and you are only mildly perplexed when those folks don't get along with one another.

Even if you're not the rebel in a group, you appreci-ate the person who stirs up trouble and says, "Why are we doing it this way?" The Capricorn side recognizes rules, but the Aquarian side says, "To heck with the rules." Folks who know you well will not be surprised at how frequently you need to remove yourself from the fray for some rest and relaxation—and your closest companions will admire you for your ability to take care of yourself.

Need some examples of folks who "set a trend"? Christian Dior (January 21), whose "new look" in the post–World War II period gave women the luxury to be ultra-feminine and powerful. Geena Davis (also January 21) was a very tall, strong-featured model who achieved a crazy trifecta in her public life: successful model, Academy Award–winning actor, and archer! George Balanchine (January 22) came from the USSR and revolutionized how dance was taught and how ballet looked. For more than a half-century, Balanchine's name and style dominated an entire performance industry, and his influence continues long after his death.

Since we're on the topic of dancing, here's another excellent role model: Chita Rivera (January 23). I got to see the one-time Dolores Conchita Figueroa del Rivero in her solo show, *Chita Rivera, The Dancer's Life*, in 2006. She was in her early seventies, but sang, danced, and told stories with an amazing energy. Here's a woman who fought her way out of the chorus line, broke a color barrier by playing the tempestuous Anita in *West Side Story*, and later was the first Latina to receive a Kennedy Center Honors award. Onstage, she was mesmerizing.

Final Thoughts

Pursue adventures—be aware of practicalities, but don't let them weigh you down. Think about the big picture, and embrace impractical dreams. You may not have an easy (or solvent) path, but your ability to lead others will make for a dazzling life. Capricorn-Aquarius is a risk taker and an individual. And though you may want to be part of the herd at times—particularly in your youth—you need to learn to listen to your heart, and follow the narrow, twisting path. "Mainstream" isn't your stream—and if it is, that's because you've changed the rules!

Times of the year when you're "on fire" and should move all projects forward

January 18–25, March 17–23, May 17–24, September 20–27, November 18–24

Times of the year when you may feel compromised or that your judgment isn't as sound as you'd like

July 20–27, October 18–24, December 18–23

chapter thirteen

AQUARIUS-PISCES CUSP

The Signs at a Glance

Aquarius and Pisces can be coming and going all at once. They are sensitive, perceptive folks who might have a touch of depression, but they still feel obligated to take care of the world. Here, Uranus brings eccentricity and electricity to Neptune's desire to escape into delusion, and Aquarius-Pisces can have (or yearn to live in) a rich fantasy life. Expressing themselves verbally (or in song or poetry) is their comfort zone, though they're probably self-conscious about this.

Dates of Transition

Aquarius finishes on February 17 or 18 and Pisces begins on February 19 or 20. If you're born on February 17, you're a Water Bearer, and if you're born on February 20, you're a Fish. Innovation meets creativity, and forward momentum collides with dithering. The dates between are a free-for-all of possibility.

Details on the Cusp Aspects

Air and water lighten up the water and make the air more grounded or substantial. Aquarius's need for freedom and fresh starts is curtailed by Pisces' nostalgic impulses. There's a dreamy aspect to this birthday—a dreamer who's aware of the relaxing properties of dreaming and letting go.

Think of Uranus and Neptune as fraternal twins. Uranus likes excitement and unpredictability. It's in charge of realms like electricity, mass trends, and freedom. Neptune likes inner freedom, and sometimes discipline is an issue (as it is with Pisces in general).

If this is your birthday zone, please, please, please take some art and meditation lessons at some point in your life path. Music counts too. There is a natural creativity that goes with this birthday, along with extreme sensitivity and perceptiveness. "Feeling hurt" is very common among people with this birthday, and it's not for me to tell you to "toughen up." I *can* advise you to use your psychological insight to explore just how others are insensitive—and then urge you to develop coping mechanisms so you don't fall into the Pisces tendency of brooding.

Those with these birthdays have an understanding and appreciation of nature along with a sense of "what's right" for humanity. You are "people" person, and a humanitarian to your core, but you won't limit yourself to one species! You're drawn to alternative sources of medicine, energy, and philosophy, and you also have the rare gift of being able to combine passions for both art and science. Idealism makes you attractive to others, but be mindful that Piscean influence wants you to procrastinate and Aquarian influence says, "Didn't we cover this? I'm bored—let's move on!"

You're comfortable with all ages, probably, but particularly the very old and the very young. You know that people at those extreme ends of their lives have a lot to share, and you're receptive to their message. At some point in your life you may be tempted to get dreadlocks—just to see if you can do it! Your logic is not the same as others' logic, and you are someone whom others want on their team. Whether you want to be on a team is up for grabs! You don't mind making sacrifices for the greater good and could have an "easy come, easy go" philosophy.

If you're born at the end of Aquarius, you'll be more sentimental about relationships than many Aquarians. You might say, "Gee, I haven't seen so and so for a while—guess I should call ...," whereas early Aquarians are more likely to say, "Gee, I haven't seen so and so for a while. Hey, what's for dinner?" You hate being called "trendy," but you definitely have a skill at anticipating what the "next big thing" might be.

If you're born at the start of Pisces, you'll be a little tougher than folks born later in the sign. You'll be more social and more likely to have friends who challenge you to grow. You love music, but meditation could make you restless.

Lovers, Partners, Friends

You are one lovable sign. Cute and quirky, deep and loving. Aquarius cusp of Pisces folks have a variety of interests, and can also have a wide range of "types." The combination of air and water makes you intense and effervescent—you need someone who will lighten up your dark side, but who has depth and complexity as well. You don't mind going along without a relationship, and you don't mind a relationship where you're not "in each other's pockets" all the time (e.g., a long-distance affair). Ultimately, however, you are very domestic, and the idea of creating a home that's a refuge is highly attractive.

Fire signs (Aries, Leo, and Sagittarius) will be exciting and could definitely "bowl you over" with their interest and passion. However, you could feel rushed when you spend time with those folks, particularly Aries or Leos. They'll have something cooking, or something that you "have to" go do, just when you're feeling like you need a break from the fray. But these folks are a lot of fun, and they will help you get out of yourself.

Earth signs (Taurus, Virgo, and Capricorn) are steady, and would also appreciate how deeply you think and feel about things. Even if they don't feel that way themselves, they'll be charmed by your take on the world. However, for a long-term partnership, you may find that their need for security, consistency, and routine is at odds with your (truly) revolutionary spirit. Virgo is opposite your Sun sign, and chances are, you will, at some point or another, need to see whether "opposites attract"!

Air signs (Gemini, Libra, and Aquarius) are good friends and definitely have the potential to be something more. But do they have the depth you want in a relationship? They may be quick to react, and you may be put in a position where you're saying, "No, I don't think I want to do *that* about that situation. I just wanted to vent!" May Geminis could "rub you the wrong way," by the way.

Water signs (Cancer, Scorpio, and Pisces) definitely "get" you. They like quirkiness and independence, and they appreciate your taste and philosophical side. They also reserve the right to be moody, and they would be happy being domestic with you, particularly Cancer. October Scorpios could be really attractive, but you might be getting the sharp end of their stinger more than you'd like.

Careers and Vocations
Aquarius-Pisces

Airlines, alternative health care, bartender, brewer, broadcasting, chemist, computers, divers, electrician or electrical field, duct cleaning, tile installation, rug sales, floral designer, work in a plant shop, custodial, pest control, radio engineer, radiology, wine maker or wine merchant.

February 15, 16, 17, 18
Aquarius, Cusp of Pisces

Independence is a hallmark of Aquarius, but Pisces (moody, mystical, privacy-loving) definitely swims among the Aquarian influence, which can leaven some self-destructive tendencies. But some get sucked under, like 1970s supermodel Margaux Hemingway (February 16). Hemingway came from humble, mostly rural surroundings, and never truly recovered from her meteoric rise.

I remember her rise to fame, because it occurred in the mid 1970s, when fresh-faced models were beginning to be edged out by less conventional beauties like Lauren Hutton, with her gap-toothed smile, and Brooke Shields, whose mature face and heavy brows set new standards for beauty. Unfortunately, Hemingway was not able to survive living in the party-hearty disco inferno. Her tragic suicide pointed to an essential lack of self-understanding.

Righteousness is a comfortable spot for you. Helping others must be the result of righteousness. Though Aquarius is truly the most independent air sign, you folks can do very well with a partner by your side. Susan B. Anthony (February 15) had great ideas, but she needed workerbee Elizabeth Cady Stanton to help further her campaign for women's suffrage. Aquarian idealism and vision has always been an important aspect of American political life, and Anthony had the communication skills to sum up the inequities for a mass audience.

There's also a peppery side. We may think of the fire signs as being hot-tempered, but Aquarius people are able to stir things up when they feel they're justified. February

16 birthdays include John McEnroe, Sonny Bono, and film director John Schlesinger, whose view on the dark side of humanity was artistically challenging and influential. I've found some of you have a desire to foment revolution because you find bliss in chaos. Some, like Huey Newton (February 17), make their mark by taking the work of others and then urging others to take action, rather than reflecting.

Okay, how about some folks whose desire for making societal change really did improve the world? Marian Anderson (February 17) broke the color barrier when she sang at the White House. Personal transformation is a huge part of Aquarius's story, and with Pisces so close, you don't mind blurring the borders, like Barry Humphries, a hard-working Australian actor who achieved international acclaim as Dame Edna Everage.

My favorite mystery novelist, Ruth Rendell (February 17), is one of the workhorses of the genre, and all of her books are polished gems. Some years ago, she developed another authorial personna, "Barbara Vine," for novels that were mysteries, but more of the psychological suspense variety. Rendell's career began in the 1960s, and her consistency as a writer is rightly celebrated. The novels written under that pen name always featured the point of view of killers, the deranged, and the sociopathic. Rendell, writing as Vine, is brilliant at getting into the heads of unusual characters and making their thought processes accessible to readers.

Sympathy for the devil (or anyone) is also a trait. You have an affinity for the "down and out" (a Pisces fascination) along with the Aquarian curiosity that says: "Why do they tick? What's important to them?" You will undoubt-edly have a rich and varied array of friends and acquain-tances because of this curiosity.

Make time to be creative, make time to recharge, and understand that folks with dark intentions may want your approval. I've never known someone in the Pisces arena (and, yes, you are truly an Aquarius, but you do have some fishies swimming in your psyche!) who didn't have friends or family members with mental problems, substance abuse issues, or behavioral kinks that didn't take to easy explana-tion. Remember: you are not in charge of other people's choices.

February 19, 20
Aquarius-Pisces Cusp

Maverick, sensitive, heedless of consequence—you're part rebel and part poet. Writer Amy Tan (February 19) is one of the more successful translators of the Asian-American experience, and her ability to juggle two worlds should be seen as emblematic. The airy nature can make for a good communicator; however the Pisces influence means com-munication won't be spoken. Although it could be poetic, rhythmic, harmonic, or kinetic.

Smokey Robinson's (February 19) voice spans so many moods and states of mind, from triumphant to tragic, ro-mantic to resigned, he could be a star within a group, or a solo star. Quirkiness continues with the February 20 birth-day folks, such as Kurt Cobain. The Aquarian elements of his story are the way his meteoric career anticipated and redefined the punk rock inheritance; the Piscean watery influence is the amount of emotion he could pack into a lyric that was basically screamed. A taste for eccentrics can be seen in Robert Altman's long film career and tendency to let actors improvise in large ensemble groups. And Patty Hearst transitioned from debutante, to kidnap victim, to defiant criminal, to prisoner, to matron, to supporting player in John Waters' cheerfully trashy film career.

Massachusetts-based Cheryl DalPozzal (February 20) is a very early Pisces who exemplifies the blending of The Water Carrier and The Fish. She works as an executive assistant to the COO of Harmonix Music, developers of Rockband. Since Pisces is musical, and Aquarius is definitely the guiding sign for new media, she's perfectly positioned to explore both signs. "I'm hoping to extend my responsibilities to a production role in the near future," she explains, adding that her Pisces traits include being "creative, intuitive, emotional." She shies away from the spotlight but doesn't mind being in it once in a while. "I prefer to work behind the scenes. I'm so happy I have a job where I am surrounded by creative and intelligent people. Although my position isn't creative per se, it does require creative problem-solving as the company has grown and developed."

Working with creative people is definitely a Pisces-Aquarius strength. Her other Pisces tendencies include teaching herself the rudiments of photography. "I am self-taught, as of 2005, and have had a few shots published. It took me a long time to actually call myself an 'artist,' since I never took that side of myself seriously. I started putting my work out there."

The Aquarian need for freedom expresses itself in her "dreamy and methodical side." "I enjoy making order out of chaos and am comfortable in working in a high stress and hectic production environment. I consider myself humanitarian in that I try to be kind to others (even strangers) and do my best to volunteer for good causes at least once a year. I've volunteered with Planned Parenthood and The Dana Farber Pan Mass Challenge."

You must make room for an artistic influence, especially of the musical variety, if you are to reach your full potential. Yes, you can be a doctor, or a lawyer, or a banker, but you have a creative flair that is going to need an outlet. Pisces is about images, and Aquarius is definitely verbal, so don't let the "verbal" or "oral" side of your communication skills drown out the side that wants to communicate without words, sentences, or paragraphs.

February 21, 22, 23, 24
Pisces, Cusp of Aquarius

Aquarian idealism and Pisces sensitivity mix harmoniously in yoga teacher and special-ed instructor Sarah Klapprodt (February 23). The Massachusetts-based mother of three has a whiteboard in her kitchen, where a selection from the "Desiderata" by poet and lawyer Max Ehrmann has been copied for morning inspiration: "Go placidly amidst the noise and haste ... be gentle with yourself ... You are a child of the universe, no less than the trees and the stars." Hopefulness and a love of music—music that's not just entertainment—have been lifelong traits. Her favorite band is Phish.

Like the Grateful Dead for the previous generation, Phish pulls together a community, not just an audience.

"When my oldest child was a year old and I was pregnant with my second child, my husband Todd and I went to a Phish Festival in Maine in the summer of 2003," she explains. "There were so many people, so much music, and it was amazing. Even though the traffic was backed up for hours, people just got out of the cars and hung out, playing games, sharing food, just being together. Once we got to the actual concert, our fellow music lovers made a dance circle so my one-year-old could dance and groove safely with the rest of us. There was nothing but love around."

For Sarah, music is the guiding spirit of her house and her heart. "I feel it in my soul, as clichéd as that sounds. There is so much sound, you are transported to magical places. The kids love it when I play it around the house—it's their 'happy jumpy' music. And when I listen to the band's earlier work, it reminds me to take a moment and live—to put the chores aside for a moment and just enjoy dancing and playing with my kids."

You want harmony, but don't want to give up your "rebel" side. You have definite ideas about the world you want to live in, and, unlike Pisces with later birthdays, you don't mind stirring things up to change the world to fit your desires. Others Pisces may look at you with awe (or dismay), but for you, the Aquarian influence is a huge help.

Pisces can wallow in real or imagined slights, or be tremendously sensitive to others. Having Aquarius so close acts as a kind of anesthesia. You may not feel that tough, but you'll come off as having a sense of what you want and who you are. And, it might be that only through exploring another culture (this is an Aquarian as well as Sagittarian interest) will you find that the world finally "makes sense."

All the folks who turned toward Eastern religions in the 1960s will probably cite Beatle George Harrison (February 25) as the avatar. When the Beatles went to India to meet with the Maharishi, it made the biggest impact on George. His interest in Indian music and culture only grew, and when he and Ravi Shankar organized The Concert for Bangladesh (1971), it was the superstar benefit, and paved the way for LiveAid and other global events.

Pisces is concerned with the downtrodden, and those less fortunate, and your Aquarian influence prompts you to take action. You're more "action-oriented" than other Pisces, and less whimsical than Aquarius. In your heart, you prefer peace to conflict, silence to ruckus. Though you may have your share of incendiary personalities in your life, in the end, you're happier on your own than many other signs.

Final Thoughts

Aquarius and Pisces combines Uranus and Neptune, hopes and wishes, dreams and fears. It's an awkward cusp, and one that you may have to "grow into." If you go through a period of your life "walking on the wild side," or being attracted to dark or destructive people or behaviors, be aware that you can always outgrow these impulses. There's a true duality in your nature, and it's one of the big divides of the psyche: To hope for the best? Or to plan for the worst? Or some combination? At your best, you can do pretty much anything. At your most challenged, procrastination will paralyze you.

Times of the year when you're "on fire" and should move all projects forward

February 15–23, April 17–23, June 18–23, September 18–24, December 17–23

Times of the year when you may feel compromised or that your judgment isn't as sound as you'd like

May 18–25, August 18–25, October 18–24

chapter fourteen

PISCES - ARIES CUSP

The Signs at a Glance

Pisces is the last sign of the zodiac, and Aries is the first sign. This combination brings us from the end to the beginning—over and over. The child (Aries) meets the crone or old man (Pisces), and they find they have more in common than they think they did. Pisces-Aries is always ready for the new day, but also eager to review or reconsider decisions of the past, to see if improvements are possible. Neptune (deception) usually succumbs to Aries' forceful tendencies—Mars's influence. Pisces-Aries needs to recharge but really would prefer not to. Full steam ahead is a default setting.

Dates of Transition

Pisces transitions to Aries on or around March 20 and 21. If you are born March 17, 18, 19, you are definitely a Pisces. If you are born March 22 and after, you are definitely an Aries. The cuspy zone could find you born under either Sun sign.

Details on the Cusp Aspects

Water and fire together can make for a steamy personality, or one that is constantly being "quenched" by circumstances, conditioning, or other people's comments. Since Pisces is a mutable sign (one that comes at the end of a season), symbolized by The Fish, with water as its ruling element, Pisces personalities can be recessive to the point of quiescent, highly sensitive, and attuned to others. Aries is a cardinal sign (one that comes at the beginning of a season), ruled by fire, with The Ram as its symbol. So we have two animals as far apart geographically as any creatures in the zodiac: the fish of the deep seas and the mountain-loving ram.

Not surprisingly, Pisces-Aries can be private and public; effusive and secretive; childlike and surprisingly mature. Since Pisces comes at the end of the zodiac, and Aries at the beginning, many Pisces seem older than their years and many Aries seem younger than their years. Your birthday also coincides with the biggest season change in the zodiacal year: winter into spring. For astrologers, this is is the "new year," when the solar cycle begins again. Thus, you find the "heaviness" (responsibilities or self-consciousness) of Pisces mixed with Aries' hope, optimism, feckless-ness and "leap before you look" inclination.

Does this make for an interesting life? Always. Coming to terms with these two deeply divided impulses—private and public, meditative and action-seeking, reclusive and extroverted—is a lifelong journey. Others will always underestimate your ability to change gears, especially if they key into the mystical Pisces influence. And you may be surprised at your own ability to adapt in relationships, fields of study, career paths, or other interests.

If you're born at the end of Pisces, you're likely more ambitious and impulsive than other Pisces. However, Aries is one of those signs that's all about leading, versus completing, so people born in this zone could have procrastination issues or that unique ability to get so far with a project and then just walk away.

If you're born at the start of Aries, you could be more tentative than Aries born later in the sign (and especially Aries-Taurus). Others may think you need encouragement. Thus you find yourself being frequently told, "Good job!" in a slightly patronizing manner. Be strategic—don't share all your plans at once, and gather your troops before making a move. Aries is known for impetuousness, but even without a measure of earth in your chart, you can learn the virtues of patience.

Lovers, Partners, Friends

You like people who take charge but are not pushy, and who are sensitive but not overly emotional. Because you have water and fire as influences, you would be drawn to those who "live large" and don't mind making a splash, but who understand the value of friends, family, and the occasional splurge.

Pisces, with its Neptune ruler, will tempt you by increasing the attractiveness of eccentric or opinionated folks. Someone who knows their own mind and is very clear about what they think would be fascinating. In part, because you have so many complicated feelings, someone who can simplify matters would be appealing and very different for you. For stability, someone with earth somewhere in their chart would have some "staying power" with you (even if you decided to move on).

A Pisces or Aries partner would probably work well. You'd have temperamental affinities in common, and you'd also feel like you could deeply share mutual experiences. A Pisces lover might be a touch melancholy at times, so learning to weather their moods would be your biggest challenge. An Aries partner would be so impulsive that you might regularly need to say, "Slow down—I thought we had decided *that*, not *this*."

Fire signs (Aries, Leo, or Sagittarius) would "feel" right, although you might not be the best fit for Leo. They'd need one-on-one intimacy, and they wouldn't always tell you. A Sagittarius could be delighted with your company, and perfectly functional away from you. Since Sagittarius is a risk taker, and, at times, a showboat, they'd need reassurance that you'd be patient with them as they pursue the next adventure.

Earth signs (Taurus, Virgo, and Capricorn) would be lucky to have you. You'd brighten their lives with your take on the world, your depth of understanding, and your artistic interests. I can see any of these signs being a good fit, but only after you've sampled a wide range of partners. Earth signs are about consistency and dependability, and Pisces-Aries doesn't always value those principles.

Air signs (Gemini, Libra, and Aquarius) would be lots of fun, very surprising, and a bit of a whirlwind in terms of jumping into the romance. Their sense of whimsy and flightiness might make you feel very grounded and solid by comparison. These are excellent folks who make excellent friends in any case, as they'd appreciate your complexities. However, you might be exhausted by the end of an evening!

Water signs (Cancer, Scorpio, and Pisces) might also feel "familiar," but ultimately too similar. Water signs all brood, and you'd want someone who could get you out of yourself. A partner who's independent, yet loyal. A Cancer partner would make for a solid and satisfying match. You'd understand one another, but you may make them crazy with your own inconsistencies and peccadilloes. Be very watchful about a partner's temper—you definitely can go off the rails, but someone too tightly wrapped might be simmering long after the heat was turned down on your argument.

Careers and Vocations
Pisces-Aries

Addiction counseling, animal care (including wildlife), antique dealer, artist, automotive industry, bartender, brewer, carpets (selling/buying/making), computers, duct cleaning, custodial work, electrician or electrical field, floral designer, guidance or career counseling, heating and furnace work, optometrist, plant shop owner, tavern keeper, tile installer, wine maker.

March 16, 17, 18, 19
Pisces, Cusp of Aries

A March 19 or 20 birthday puts you at the end of Pisces. What does it mean to be born at the end of the end of the signs? Generally, this is a how-tough-do-I-have-to-be birthday, and those born on these days have both sensitivity and a realism about (the worst possible way) the world can work. Pisces is always a droll sign—you're old when you're young. I've seen lots of folks who have interesting family circumstances which bring out Pisces' caretaking side. If you've had more than the usual amount of responsibility (careless, heedless, or thoughtless siblings; parents who didn't have their act together), you're probably tougher than you think you are.

Legendary modern-day movie mogul Harvey Weinstein and award-winning dramatist Neil LaBute (*The Company of Men*, *Fat Pig*) share a March 19 birthday. Both men, it can be argued, are tougher than old boots when it comes to seeing all the angles. Miramax, the film company Weinstein ran with his brother Bob, was the independent success story of the 1980s and 1990s. The pair parlayed smart purchases into box office boffo. After it won the Palme d'Or prize at Cannes in 1989, Miramax expanded and had greater cultural influence, arguably, than any film production company since the great age of the Hollywood studio system.

It is interesting to note that some of Pisces' themes or concerns—prisons, secrets, incarceration, subconscious motives, sexual anxiety—are reflected in the early Miramax hits: Errol Morris's *The Thin Blue Line*, for example, or *Sex, Lies, and Videotape*. One wouldn't think these topics would have mainstream appeal, but when Pisces follows their natural instincts, the way that Weinstein has, the world has a way of catching up.

As for LaBute, he's been celebrated and deplored for his less-than-flattering portraits of the human condition, yet acknowledged as one of the gifted playwrights for his generation. A master of realistic dialogue (à la David Mamet), he is fascinated with the disintegration of human relationships. I had the opportunity to speak to him before the Boston premiere of his 2003 drama, *Fat Pig*, a play about a heavyset woman having a relationship with a man who sees her true inner beauty—for a while. "It was fun for me and interesting to write about something that's starting," LaBute said. "Usually, [relationships in my work] have existed for a while and I'm about to make it wither. It was different watching the courtship and the beginnings of the relationship."

Never let it be said that March 19 people lack endurance. Both Ursula Andress, born 1936, and Glenn Close, born 1947, have had long careers as mysterious cinematic sexpots. Turning forty or fifty, and beyond, has been no impediment to their success!

March 20, 21
Pisces-Aries Cusp

March 20 cusp really is the edge of the edge, but Aries can imbue you with confidence and leadership abilities. You have perception and sensitivity, but also restlessness that propels you forward. You're capable of enormous confidence and vacillating self-doubt. I've seen clients and friends wrestle with these two opposing forces over and over. Passion comes easily, but you may also be put off by people who are "too intense," or who have lots of emotional difficulties. Pisces' droll dark humor is lightened by Aries' childlike honesty and wanting to make everything simple.

Filmmakers Carl Reiner and Spike Lee share a March 20 birthday, along with legendary NBA coach Pat Riley. There's a visionary element that goes with all Pisces; and in the case of Lee, at least once a decade, he produces a movie that prompts a widespread discussion on cultural issues. If you're a March 20 person, your nervous system will definitely operate at a higher rev than those of your Pisces counterparts born just days before! You are fairly graceful in your movements, but you definitely can suffer from a case of "the blurts" (a fire-sign weakness). When you are being honest with others, work on answering this question: "Am I being a little bit rude?"

Johann Sebastian Bach was born March 21, 1685. He was an Aries who puts most people to shame when it comes to productivity and activity. A master of the contrapuntal technique, which was regarded as increasingly old-fashioned as he matured, Bach's compositional talents and skills as an organist were noted early on. Precocity is one hallmark of Aries. Bach came from a musical family and was the patriarch of many musicians and composers (Carl Philipp Emanuel and Wilhelm Friedemann). Aries people can have a revolutionary side, but those born so close to Pisces will always have a taste for traditional forms and patterns.

Blues-gospel singer "King" Solomon Burke is another March 21 birthday boy who showed early promise. His career has taken him from the ministry to road shows to movies to interesting collaborations with other artists. His fluency in a variety of styles (rock, blues, country, gospel, jazz) shows authentic Aries curiosity and fearlessness. Aries folks enjoy a challenge and also thrive in partnerships in which their own gifts are appreciated. And when you throw a tantrum, it's theatrical and self-conscious. Being aware of how others react keeps one foot (or fin, or hoof!) in reality.

Speaking of challenge and versatility, consider Rosie O'Donnell (March 21). She's one of those versatile performers who can seemingly do anything and remain "likable." Her successful standup career brought her interesting movie roles and paved the way for her first talk-show and then (short-lived) lifestyle magazine, *Rosie*. Her decision to come out about her sexual orientation stirred up far less controversy than Ellen DeGeneres's similar decision in the 1990s.

You folks have a big advantage in that others may underestimate you because of your youthful affect. This means you can have the upper hand because everything you say sounds a little bit brilliant. "Enfant terrible" is a comfortable role—and one that amuses the rest of us to no end!

Others also may underestimate your ability to laugh at yourself and to rise above hardship. Though it may take you a while to decide "what you feel," the happiest Pisces-Aries are curious about others and able to put their own needs aside often enough to be a helpful member of society. Your insights into a wide range of people are worth listening to, and your intuitive abilities, especially when it concerns the "forgotten" members of society (elderly, imprisoned, disabled, or otherwise incapacitated) are strong. You are able to simplify complicated situations with style, and your artistic inclinations can be as strong as scientific impulses.

March 22, 23, 24, 25
Aries, Cusp of Pisces

Courage, curiosity, and clout. You may give the impression to others that you're persuadable, but the bottom line is that you're going to follow your own instincts—and others should be grateful. That's okay, because you know what you want. Broadway impressario-composer Andrew Lloyd Webber (March 22) has some classic Aries juice—hey, he did reinvent the Broadway musical. He is a genius in his ability to transform an older theme into something modern and cutting-edge. Consider how *Madame Butterfly* was incorporated into the story of *Miss Saigon*, the updating of *The Phantom of the Opera*, and his rock-musical adaptations of stories from the Old and New Testaments.

As for March 23 birthdays, quirky actor Amanda Plummer, the daughter of Christopher Plummer and Tammy Grimes, carved out a career for herself as a slightly-tetched idiot savant. Capable of playing a wide variety of mental and emotional characteristics, Plummer, in her fifties, is virtually ageless. She is the same will-o'-the-wisp eccentric she's been since her teen years. Football star Ron Jaworski is also an Aries who was smart when it came to changing his pro team (Rams, Eagles, Dolphins, and Chiefs). Then in post-retirement, he has remade himself as a charming broadcaster. Aries people, cuspy or not, are happily outspoken, as March 24 birthday folk such as Star Jones would agree. And early retirement can suit Aries—just talk to billionaire Microsoft exec Steve Ballmer.

And, yes, there's temperament. Aries cusp of Pisces can range from volatile (Ballmer, Joan Crawford, Lara Flynn Boyle) to the determined, yet outwardly cool (Steve McQueen and filmmaker Akira Kurasawa). A historical figure who combines the most interesting flavors of Pisces and Aries is Harry Houdini (March 24). A magician who became a folk icon and then a generic term, Houdini updated ancient tricks and brought an element of risk to the performance that left audiences at the turn of the last century thrilled and dazed. Having an appreciation of ancient arts is a Pisces characteristic, while taking risks is definitely an Aries pursuit.

Lawrence Ferlinghetti (March 24) is another excellent example of an avatar of modernism. He was allied with the Beats, and a contemporary of Jack Kerouac, Allen Ginsberg, and other writing rebels. But he quickly figured out that "owning the shop" (the City Lights bookstore in San Francisco, which was also a publishing house) was the best route to stability. Plus, his lifelong interest in Eastern spiritual practices, back when no one outside of academia knew what Zen was, puts him into that "Aries forerunner" category.

Tasia V. is in her thirties, and a real-estate appraiser. Just over the line as an Aries (March 23), she exlains, "I always introduce myself as an Aries on the cusp of Pisces with a Pisces Moon." Despite the Neptunian influence, Aries wins out with Tasia. "I am very headstrong and impatient. I am often misunderstood for being argumentative. I have a hard time being calm when I am being told 'what to do, and how to do it.' My mother actually has a baby photo of me where I have a very angry expression on my face and my hands are balled into fists. Also, the very first time she took me to the dentist, I bit him."

Other Aries traits she's learned to recognize: "When I feel I am being pressured to do something that doesn't feel comfortable, I have a hard time and usually need to vent about it. I am getting better at being less short-tempered—this has mellowed with age. I am very good at starting new hobbies, projects, etc., but have a hard time finishing them 100 percent."

Yet her Aries side has brought professional advantages. "I've learned that people gravitate to me in organizational settings because I am outspoken and speak up when something doesn't feel right to me. I am very open with most people whom I meet and communicate with in a direct manner. You always know where you stand with me. I love to argue, but not to fight—more like debate. I often say that I should have been a lawyer."

Ultimately, Tasia views her Pisces traits as strengths. "I have a strong sense of compassion and have learned to become more patient when dealing with people and their emotional quirks." Still, she feels "cuspy" more than any sign in particular. "I feel like I have two sides—and they don't blend together. In each moment, I am either one or the other—Aries or Pisces."

She identifies with both Pisces and Aries friends—people who might not have a lot in common—and she also has many people in her life who share the trait of being born "on the edge." "I also find that there are several other cusps in my life who are very close to me … my boyfriend who is Scorpio-Sagittarius, my best friend, who is Gemini-Cancer, my mother, an Aquarius-Pisces, and another good friend who is a Sagittarius-Capricorn."

Final Thoughts

Pisces-Aries can embrace the best of both signs. Use your Pisces sensitivity to explore what others are thinking and feeling and be grateful you won't be paralyzed by typically fishie shyness or over-involvement in others' feelings. Your Aries influence will help you get things going, and get moving when you need to. If you have to work a little bit harder at completing projects, always look for collaboration. Aries folks are meant to be leaders, which never means you do things on your own. Just that you're at the front of the line!

Times of the year when you're "on fire" and should move all projects forward

January 17–24, March 17–24, May 18–25, July 20–27, October 20–27

Times of the year when you may feel compromised or that your judgment isn't as sound as you'd like

June 19–25, September 20–26, December 21–26

CUSPY BIRTHDAYS
AT A GLANCE

Here is a motley collection of actors, athletes, activists, writers, rebels and teachers, saints and sinners. I scoured my records to create a widely varied list, so those of you who find it distasteful to share a birthday with Rasputin can also delight in the immortal tunes of birthday mate Sam Cooke. I have started this list with January birthdays, which will be more convenient for most readers. And, I extended the definition of "cusp" by a day or two for all signs. I have lots of clients, friends, and family members who show distinct "flavoring" from the adjacent sign. See if you do too! These are listed alphabetically by first name and there is a line space after every birthday so you can fill in your own collection of cuspy birthdays.

January 15: Ari Onassis, Benjamin Franklin, Charo, Edward Teller, Gene Krupa, Lloyd Bridges, Margaret O'Brien, Martin Luther King Jr., Molière, Osip Mandelstam

January 16: Aaliyah, Debbie Allen, Dian Fossey, Ethel Merman, Francisco Scavullo, Kate Moss, Susan Sontag, William Kennedy

January 17: Anne Bronte, Betty White, James Earl Jones, Konstantin Stanislavski, Nevil Shute, Sheree North, Vidal Sassoon

January 18: A. A. Milne, Cary Grant, Daniel Webster, Danny Kaye, Jane Horrocks, Kevin Costner, Oliver Hardy

January 19: Dolly Parton, Edgar Allan Poe, Janis Joplin, Patricia Highsmith, Phil Everly, Robert E. Lee, Robert McNeil, Simon Rattle

January 20: Carol Heiss, David Lynch, Edwin "Buzz" Aldrin, Federico Fellini, George Burns, Patricia Neal, Ruth St. Denis

January 21: Christian Dior, Geena Davis, Jack Nicklaus, Paul Scofield, Placido Domingo, Richie Havens, Telly Savalas

January 22: August Strindberg, D. W. Griffith, Francis Bacon, George Balanchine, Jeff Mosser, John Hurt, Linda Blair, Lord Byron, Rasputin, Sam Cooke

January 23: Anita Pointer, Chita Rivera, Django Reinhardt, Gary Burton, Humphrey Bogart, John Hancock, Sergei Eisenstein, Stendhal

January 24: Edith Wharton, Ernest Borgnine, E. T. A. Hoffman, John Belushi, Nastassja Kinski, Robert Motherwell, Sharon Tate, Warren Zevon

February 15: Alfred North Whitehead, Claire Bloom, Ernest Shackleton, Jane Seymour, Jeremy Bentham, John Barrymore, Matt Groening, Melissa Manchester, Susan B. Anthony

February 16: Edgar Bergen, Henry Adams, John McEnroe, John Schlesinger, LeVar Burton, Margaux Hemingway, Sonny Bono

February 17: Alan Bates, Chaim Potok, Lou Diamond Phillips, Huey Newton, Marian Anderson, Michael Jordan, Ruth Rendell

February 18: Andre Breton, Cybill Shepherd, Helen Gurley Brown, John Travolta, Matt Dillon, Milos Forman, Molly Ringwald, Sholem Aleichem, Toni Morrison

February 19: Amy Tan, Andre Breton, Prince Andrew, Carson McCullers, Justine Bateman, Lee Marvin, Merle Oberon, Smokey Robinson

February 20: Ansel Adams, Cheryl DalPozza, Buffy St. Marie, Ivana Trump, Patty Hearst, Robert Altman, Russel Crouse, Sandy Duncan, Sidney Poitier, Kurt Cobain

February 21: Anais Nin, Barbara Jordan, Erma Bombeck, Hubert de Givenchy, John Henry Newman, Rue McClanahan, Tyne Daly, Sam Peckinpah, W. H. Auden

February 22: Drew Barrymore, Edna St. Vincent Millay, George Washington, James Russell Lowell, Luis Bunuel, Julius Erving ("Dr. J"), Sean O'Faolain, Sybil Leek

February 23: Aziz Ansari, Dakota Fanning, Johnny Winter, Peter Fonda, Sarah Klapprodtk, Samuel Pepys, Victor Fleming, W. E. B. Du Bois

February 24: Eddie Murphy, Edward James Olmos, Enrico Caruso, George Thorogood, Kristin Davis, Steve Jobs, Wilhelm Grimm, Winslow Homer

February 25: Anthony Burgess, George Harrison, Jim Backus, John Foster Dulles, Pierre Auguste Renoir, Sean Astin, Sally Jessy Raphael, Tom Courtenay, Zeppo Marx

March 16: Daniel Patrick Moynihan, Henny Youngman, Isabelle Huppert, James Madison, Jerry Lewis, Kate Nelligan, Mercedes McCambridge, Pat Nixon

March 17: Bobby Jones, Gary Sinese, John Sebastian, Kate Greenaway, Kurt Russell, Mia Hamm, Nat "King" Cole, Rob Lowe, Rudolph Nureyev

March 18: Bonnie Blair, Charlie Pride, Edgar Cayce, F. W. de Klerk, Grover Cleveland, Irene Cara, John Updike, Queen Latifah, Peter Graves, Vanessa Williams, Wilson Pickett

March 19: Bruce Willis, Harvey Weinstein, Glenn Close, Irving Wallace, Moms Mabley, Neil LaBute, Philip Roth, Serge Diaghilev, Ursula Andress, Wyatt Earp

March 20: B. F. Skinner, Bobby Orr, Carl Reiner, Fred "Mr." Rogers, Hal Linden, Henrik Ibsen, Holly Hunter, Ozzie Nelson, Pat Riley, Spike Lee, William Hurt

March 21: Johann Sebastian Bach, Gary Oldman, "King" Solomon Burke, Matthew Broderick, Modeste Mussorgsky, Robert the Bruce, Rosie O'Donnell, Timothy Dalton

March 22: Andrew Lloyd Webber, Chico Marx, Elvis Stojko, George Benson, Marcel Marceau, Matthew Modine, Pat Robertson, Stephen Sondheim, William Shatner

March 23: Akira Kurosawa, Amanda Plummer, Chaka Khan, Eric Idle, Erich Fromm, Joan Crawford, Keri Russell, Moses Malone, Ron Jaworski, Werner Von Braun

March 24: Bob Mackie, Clyde Barrow, Harry Houdini, Lara Flynn Boyle, Lawrence Ferlinghetti, Star Jones, Steve Ballmer, Steve McQueen, Wilhelm Reich

March 25: Aretha Franklin, Arturo Toscannini, Bela Bartok, Debi Thomnas, Ed Begley, Elton John, Flannery O'Conner, Howard Cosell, Sarah Jessica Parker, Simone Signoret

April 15: Bessie Smith, Claudia Cardinale, Elizabeth Montgomery, Harold Washington, Jeffrey Archer, Roy Clark, Thomas Hart Benton

April 16: Charlie Chaplin, Ellen Barkin, Henry Mancini, Herbie Mann, Merce Cunningham, Peter Ustinov, Spike Milligan, Wilbur Wright

April 17: J. P. Morgan, Nikita Kruschev, Isak Dinesen, Don Kirschner, Harry Reasoner, Huntington Hartford, Lindsay Anderson, Thornton Wilder, William Holden

April 18: America Ferrera, Clarence Darrow, Conan O'Brien, Eric Roberts, Hayley Mills, James Woods, Melissa Joan Hart

April 19: Don Adams, Dudley Moore, Harold Lloyd, Jayne Mansfield, Lionel Hampton, Lucrezia Borgia, Paloma Picasso, Suzie Kowaleski

April 20: Adolf Hitler, Carmen Electra, Jessica Lange, Joan Miro, Lionell Hampton, Luther Vandross, Ryan O'Neal, Sarah E. Collins, Tito Puente

April 21: Anthony Quinn, Charlotte Bronte, Elaine May, Queen Elizabeth, John Mortimer, John Muir, Norman Parkinson, Patti Lupone, Tony Danza

April 22: Charles Mingus, Glen Campbell, Henry Fielding, Immanuel Kant, Jack Nicholson, Lenin, Robert Oppenheimer

April 23: Max Planck, Ngaio Marsh, Roy Orbison, Sandra Dee, Shirley Temple, Stephen A. Douglas, Valerie Bertinelli, Vladimir Nabokov, William Shakespeare

April 24: Anthony Trollope, Barbra Streisand, Richard M. Daley Jr., Robert Penn Warren, Shirley MacLaine, Willem de Kooning

May 16: Billy Martin, Billy Cobham, Christian Lacroix, Debra Winger, Henry Fonda, Janet Jackson, Pierce Brosnan, Tori Spelling, Woody Herman

May 17: Archibald Cox, Craig Ferguson, Dennis Hopper, Dewey Redman, Enya, Jordan Knight, Sugar Ray Leonard, Trent Reznor

May 18: Bertrand Russell, Bill Macy, Frank Capra, Dame Margot Fonteyn, Nicholas II, Perry Como, Pierre Balmain, Rick Wakeman, Tina Fey

May 19: Grace Jones, Honoré de Balzac, Jim Lehrer, Joey Ramone, Malcolm X, Lady Nancy Astor, Nora Ephron, Pete Townshend

May 20: Bronson Pinchot, Busta Rhymes, Cher, Jimmy Stewart, Joe Cocker, John Stewart Mill, Moshe Dayan

May 21: Richard Wagner, Fats Waller, Raymond Burr, Andre Sakharov, Alexander Pope, Harold Robbins, Christine Robert, Robert Creeley

May 22: Arthur Conan Doyle, Harvey Milk, Laurence Olivier, Mary Cassatt, Paul Winfield, Richard Wagner, T-Bone Walker

May 23: Carolus Linnaeus, Joan Collins, Margaret Fuller, Marvin Hagler, Robert Moog, Rosemary Clooney

June 18: E.G. Marshall, Isabella Rossellini, Jeanette MacDonald, Paul McCartney, Philip Barry, Sylvia Porter

June 19: AJ Wachtel, Alan Cranston, Blase Pascal, Gena Rowlands, Kathleen Turner, Kay Williams Graves, Lou

Gehrig, Malcolm McDowell, Moe Howard, Paula Abdul, Wallis Simpson

June 20: Audie Murphy, Chet Akins, Cyndi Lauper, Danny Aiello, Errol Flynn, Lillian Hellman, Nicole Kidman

June 21: Francoise Sagan, Jean-Paul Sartre, Judy Holliday, Jane Russell, Mary McCarthy, Nils Lofgren, Rockwell Kent, Prince William

June 22: Anne Morrow Lindbergh, Bill Blass, Billy Wilder, Diane Feinstein, Erich Maria Remarque, Joseph Papp, Kris Kristofferson, Meryl Streep, Tracy Pollan

June 23: Alfred Kinsey, Bob Fosse, Clarence Thomas, Edward VIII (Duke of Windsor), Jean Anouilh, Richard Bach, Wilma Rudolph

July 18: Clifford Odets, Elizabeth McGovern, Dr. Hunter S. Thompson, John Glenn, Nelson Mandela, William Makepeace Thackeray, Yevgeny Yevtushenko

July 19: A.J. Cronin, Charles Mayo, Edgar Degas, George McGovern, Herbert Marcuse, Ilie Nastase, Lizzie Borden

July 20: Sir Edmund Hillary, Carlos Santana, Diana Rigg, Natalie Wood, Jeff Van Amburgh, Laszlo Moholy-Nagy, Theda Bara, Thomas Berger

July 21: Cat Stevens, Don Knotts, Ernest Hemingway, Hart Crane, Jon Lovitz, Jonathan Miller, Robin Williams

July 22: Albert Brooks, Alex Trebek, Danny Glover, Edward Hopper, Gregor Mendel, Jason Robards, Oscar de la Renta, Raymond Chandler, Robert Dole, Stephen Vincent Benet, Willem Dafoe

July 23: Anthony M. Kennedy, Emil Janning, Don Drysdale, Haile Selassie, Tami Heide, Woody Harrelson

July 24: Alexandre Dumas, Pere, Amelia Earhart, Bella Abzug, Franz Wedekind, Lynda Carter, Robert Graves, Zelda Fitzgerald

July 25: Annie Ross, David Belasco, Elias Canetti, Estelle Getty, Iman, Omar Khayyam, Thomas Eakins

July 26: Aldous Huxley, Blake Edwards, C. G. Jung, George Bernard Shaw, Gracie Allen, D.W. Griffith, Mick Jagger, Stanley Kubrick

August 17: Davy Crockett, Larry Rivers, Mae West, Maureen O'Hara, Robert DeNiro, Roman Polanski, Samuel Goldwyn, Sean Penn, V. S. Naipaul

August 18: Antonio Salieri, Martin Mull, Max Factor, Meriweather Lewis, Patrick Swayze, Robert Redford, Robertson Davies, Rosalynn Carter, Shelley Winters

August 19: Bill Clinton, Coco Chanel, Gene Roddenberry, Jill St. John, John Stamos, Ogden Nash, Orville Wright, Peter Gallagher, Ring Lardner Jr.

August 20: Connie Chung, Edgar A. Guest, Eero Saarinen, H. P. Lovecraft, Jack Teagarden, Jacqueline Susann

August 21: Count Basie, Joe Strummer, Kenny Rogers, Kim Cattrall, Princess Margaret, X. J. Kennedy

August 22: Bill Parcells, Carl Yastrzemski, Cindy Williams, Dorothy Parker, Leni Riefenstahl, Norman Schwarzkopf, Valerie Harper

August 23: Barbara Eden, Edgar Lee Masters, Ernie Bushmiller, Gene Kelly, Keith Moon, Queen Noor, River Phoenix, Shelley Long, Vera Miles

August 24: Deng Ziao Ping, Cal Ripken Jr., Jean Rhys, Jorge Luis Borges, Marlee Matlin, Max Beerbohm, Robert Herrick, Yasser Arafat

August 25: Althea Gibson, Bret Harte, Clara Bow, Gene Simmons, Leonard Bernstein, Lola Montez, Sean Connery

August 26: Ben Bradlee, Branford Marsalis, Christopher Isherwood, Geraldine Ferraro, Macauley Culkin

August 27: Bob Kerrey, Samuel Goldwyn, Ira Levin, Mother Teresa, Theodore Dreiser, Sri Chimnoy, Tuesday Weld

September 20: Alannah Curie, Donald Hall, Dr. Joyce Brothers, Red Auerbach, Sophia Loren, Stevie Smith, Upton Sinclair

September 21: Bill Murray, H. G. Wells, Larry Hagman, Leonard Cohen, Ricki Lake, Shirley Conran, Stephen King

September 22: Erich Von Stroheim, Fay Weldon, Joan Jett, John Houseman, Scott Baio, Thea Singer, Tommy Lasorda

September 23: Bruce Springsteen, John Coltrane, Julio Iglesias, Mickey Rooney, Ray Charles, Romy Schneider, Walter Lippman

September 24: Anthony Newley, Cheryl Crawford, F. Scott Fitzgerald, Jim Henson, Joseph P. Kennedy II, Linda McCartney, Phil Hartman

September 25: Barbara Walters, Cheryl Tiegs, Christopher Reeve, Heather Locklear, Mark Hamill, Mark Rothko, Michael Douglas, William Faulkner

October 18: Chuck Berry, George C. Scott, Jesse Helms, Lotte Lenya, Peter Boyle, Martina Navratilova, Melina Mercouri, Pierre Trudeau, Wendy Wasserstein, Winton Marsalis

October 19: Auguste Lumiere, Divine, Evander Holyfield, John le Carré, John Lithgow, Patricia Ireland, Peter Max, Peter Tosh

October 20: Art Buchwald, Arthur Rimbaud, Bela Lugosi, Jelly Roll Morton, Margaret Dumont, Mickey Mantle, Tom Petty

October 21: Alfred Nobel, Benjamin Netanyahu, Carrie Fisher, Dizzy Gillespie, Georg Solti, Samuel Taylor Coleridge, Simon Grey, Ted Shawn, Ursula K. Le Guin

October 22: Lord Alfred Douglas, Annette Funicello, Bobby Seale, Brian Boitano, Catherine Deneuve, Doris Lessing, Franz Liszt, Robert Rauschenberg

October 23: Diana Dors, Doug Flutie, Emily Kimbrough, Gertrude Ederle, Johnny Carson, Michael Crichton, Pelé

October 24: The Big Bopper, Bill Wyman, Denise Levertov, F. Murray Abraham, Kevin Kline, Moss Hart, Sybil Thorndike

October 25: Abel Ganz, Anne Tyler, Bobby Brown, George Bizet, Helen Reddy, John Berryman, Klaus Barbie, Marion Ross, Pablo Picasso

October 26: Francois Mitterand, Hillary Clinton, Jaclyn Smith, Mahalia Jackson, Mohammed Reza Pahlavi, Pat Sajak

October 27: Dylan Thomas, John Cleese, Nanette Fabray, Roy Lichtenstein, Ruby Dee, Sylvia Plath, Teddy Roosevelt

November 18: Elizabeth Perkins, Don Cherry, Eugene Ormandy, George Gallup, Ignace Jan Paderewski, Imogene Coca, Linda Evans, Louis Daguerre, W. S. Gilbert

November 19: Billy Strayhorn, Dick Cavett, Indira Gandhi, Jodie Foster, Martin Luther, Meg Ryan, J. R. Capablanca, Roy Campanella, Ted Turner, Wilma P. Mankiller

November 20: Alistair Cooke, Bo Derek, Dick Smothers, Duane Allman, Joseph Biden, Meredith Monk, Nadine

Gordimer, Robert C. Bird, Robert F. Kennedy, Sir Samuel Cunard

November 21: Coleman Hawkins, Goldie Hawn, Harold Ramis, Marilyn French, Marlo Thomas, Nicollette Sheridan, Rene Magritte

November 22: Andre Gide, Billie Jean King, Boris Becker, Charles de Gaulle, Dorie Clark, George Eliot, George Gissing, Sir Peter Hall, Jamie Lee Curtis, Terry Gilliam

November 23: Billy the Kid, Boris Karloff, Bruce Hornsby, Charles Berlitz, Erte, Franklin Pierce, Harpo Marx, Johnny Mandel, Miley Cyrus

November 24: Frances Hodson Burnett, Garson Kanin, Katherine Heigl, Scott Joplin, Toulouse Lautrec, William F. Buckley, Jr.

November 25: Jenna and Barbara Bush, Christina Applegate, John Larroquette, Leonard Woolf, Paul Desmond, Ricardo Montalban, Virgil Thompson

December 18: Betty Grable, Brad Pitt, Christina Aguilera, Katie Holmes, Keith Richards, Leonard Maltin, Ossie Davis, Stephen Spielberg

December 19: Alyssa Milano, Cicely Tyson, David Susskind, Jake Gyllenhaal, Jean Genet, Jennifer Beals, Sir Ralph Richardson, Richard Leakey

December 20: Billy Bragg, Branch Rickey, David Cook, George Roy Hill, Irene Dunne, Jenny Agutter, Peter Criss, Uri Geller

December 21: Anthony Powell, Benjamin Disraeli, Florence Griffeth Joyner, Frank Zappa, Heinrich Boll, Jane Fonda, Kiefer Sutherland, Phil Donahue, Ray Romano, Tim D'Onfro

December 22: Deems Taylor, Diane Sawyer, Edwin Arlington Robinson, Gene Rayburn, Giacomo Puccini, Joe Pyne, Kenneth Rexroth, Lynne Thigpen, Maurice and Robin Gibb

December 23: Carla Bruni, Madame C. J. Walker, Corey Haim, Eddie Vedder, Harry Shearer, Robert Bly, Susan Lucci

December 24: Ava Gardner, Kit Carson, Howard Hughes, Mary Higgins Clark, Matthew Arnold, Ricky Martin, Ryan Seacrest, Tycho Brahe

December 25: Annie Lennox, Carlos Castaneda, Humphrey Bogart, Joseph Smith, Quentin Crisp, Rebecca West, Rod Serling, Shane McGowan, Sissy Spacek

To Write to the Author

If you wish to contact the author or would like more information about this book, please write to the author in care of Llewellyn Worldwide Ltd. and we will forward your request. Both the author and the publisher appreciate hearing from you and learning of your enjoyment of this book and how it has helped you. Llewellyn Worldwide Ltd. cannot guarantee that every letter written to the author can be answered, but all will be forwarded. Please write to:

Sally Cragin
℅ Llewellyn Worldwide
2143 Wooddale Drive
Woodbury, MN 55125-2989

Please enclose a self-addressed stamped envelope for reply, or $1.00 to cover costs. If outside the U.S.A., enclose an international postal reply coupon.

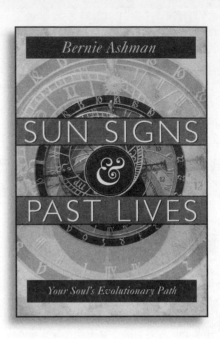

Bernie Ashman

SUN SIGNS
&
PAST LIVES

Your Soul's Evolutionary Path

Sun Signs & Past Lives
Your Soul's Evolutionary Path

BERNIE ASHMAN

Discover how to break free from destructive past-life patterns and reach your full potential.

Sun Signs & Past Lives offers an easy, foolproof way to pinpoint behaviors that may be holding you back from a rewarding life of peace and fulfillment. All you need to know is your birthday. Bernie Ashman divides each Sun sign into three energy zones, allowing easy access to innate strengths and the spiritual lessons for this lifetime. With his guidance, you'll discover how to transform these precious insights into action—reverse negative past-life tendencies, find healing, discover your life purpose, and get back on the road to empowerment.

978-0-7387-2107-1, 264 pp., 6 x 9 $16.95

To order, call 1-877-NEW-WRLD
Prices subject to change without notice
Order at Llewellyn.com 24 hours a day, 7 days a week!

The Astrological Elements
How Fire, Earth, Air & Water
Influence Your Life

SALLY CRAGIN

Are you curious about the work habits of your new Pisces co-worker? Will sparks fly with that cute Aries down the street? There is a way to find out the impulses, desires, interests, communication styles, and personalities of the people around you—Sun sign astrology!

Fun and easy to use, *The Astrological Elements* explores all twelve Sun signs through the four elements—fire, earth, air, and water—with a focus on love, work, friends, and family. Learn how to speak the language of each sign. Find out what each sign is like as a friend, boss, lover, and more. Discover the compatibility potential for each pairing and see how "neighbor" signs get along with each other. Sprinkled throughout are chart analysis examples of famous couples such as Elizabeth Taylor and Richard Burton, Demi Moore and Bruce Willis, and others.

978-0-7387-1871-2, 216 pp., 6 x 9 $18.95

To order, call 1-877-NEW-WRLD
Prices subject to change without notice
Order at Llewellyn.com 24 hours a day, 7 days a week!

Discover Your Psychic Type
Developing and Using Your Natural Intuition
SHERRIE DILLARD

Intuition and spiritual growth are indelibly linked, according to professional psychic and therapist Sherrie Dillard. Offering a personalized approach to psychic development, this breakthrough guide introduces four different psychic types and explains how to develop the unique spiritual capabilities of each.

Are you a physical, mental, emotional, or spiritual intuitive? Take Dillard's insightful quiz to find out. Discover more about each type's intuitive nature, personality, potential physical weaknesses, and more. There are guided meditations for each kind of intuitive, as well as exercises to hone your psychic skills. Remarkable stories from the author's professional life illustrate the incredible power of intuition and its connection to the spirit world, inner wisdom, and your higher self.

From psychic protection to spirit guides to mystical states, Dillard offers guidance as you evolve toward the final destination of every psychic type: union with the Divine.

978-0-7387-1278-9, 288 pp., 5³⁄₁₆ x 8   **$14.95**